Discipleship

Discipleship

Peter Maiden

Keswick
ministries
bringing the Word alive

Authentic

MILTON KEYNES ● COLORADO SPRINGS ● HYDERABAD

13 12 11 10 09 08 07   8 7 6 5 4 3 2
Reprinted 2007

First published 2007 by Keswick Ministries and Authentic Media
9 Holdom Avenue, Bletchley, Milton Keynes, Bucks,
MK1 1QR, UK
1820 Jet Stream Drive, Colorado Springs, USA
OM Authentic Media, Jeedimetla Village
Secunderabad 500 055, A.P., India
www.authenticmedia.co.uk

Authentic Media is a division of IBS-STL U.K., limited by guarantee, with its
Registered Office at Kingstown Broadway, Carlisle, Cumbria CA3 0HA.
Registered in England & Wales No. 1216232. Registered charity 270162

British Library Cataloguing in Publication Data
A catalogue record for this book is available from the British
Library
ISBN-13: 978-1-84227-762-4

Unless otherwise stated, Scripture quotations are from the Holy Bible, NEW
INTERNATIONAL VERSION®. Copyright © 1973, 1978, 1984 International
Bible Society. All rights reserved throughout the world. Used by permission
of International Bible Society.
Words from the Servant King are by Graham Kendrick
Copyright (c) 1983 Thankyou Music/Adm. by
worshiptogether.com songs
excl. UK & Europe, adm. by kingswaysongs.com
tym@kingsway.co.uk Used by Permission

Cover design David Smart
Print Management by Adare Carwin
Printed in Great Britain by J.H. Haynes & Co., Sparkford

The book is dedicated to my wife Win, who has lived out the principles of discipleship in ways that I can constantly only stand back and admire.

Contents

Part 4 What is it all for?

Part 5 It's impossible!

Series Preface

For over 130 years, the Keswick Convention has played a vital role in the growth of the worldwide evangelical faith. However, there are millions of Christians who honour the name of Keswick but have limited appreciation of the Convention's core values and commitments. This exciting new series attempts to address that gap in understanding.

By providing key studies into some of the major emphases of the Convention, the prayer of its Trustees is that a new generation will be inspired afresh, in the words of its motto, to be 'all one in Christ Jesus'. Accordingly, other titles planned for the series, to name but a few, will cover the Lordship of Christ, the work of the Spirit, the centrality of the Cross, the meaning of holiness and the call to mission and service.

Appropriately, this first title on *Discipleship* comes from the respected pen of the Chair of the Keswick Convention, Peter Maiden. Those who are 'all *one* in Christ' need to be 'all for Jesus' too. Here's how.

Welcome to 'Keswick Values.'

Steve Brady, Series Editor

Acknowledgements

This has been written in the early and late hours of the day, and on many flights and train journeys. I asked my editor, Ali Hull, to nag me until it was finished. She's good! Seriously, it would never have been completed without her help and that of my PA, Christine Ross.

Introduction

The case for the defence

Why do we need another book on discipleship? Two things which I've read and one thing I've seen in recent months have finally got me to put fingers to computer to write this book. Ron Sider wrote a book *The scandal of the evangelical conscience*. Using research produced mainly by George Barna, he showed the spiritual schizophrenia so evident in much of twenty-first century American Christianity. Divorce is slightly more evident in the church than outside of it.[1] The people most likely to object to a neighbour of a different ethnic origin are white evangelicals.[2] These were just two of a number of statistics which left me deeply disturbed and with fundamental questions. But this is not just an American or even just a western problem. The genocide in Rwanda, in which nine hundred thousand people

> ❧❦❧
>
> **The people most likely to object to a neighbour of a different ethnic origin are white evangelicals.**
>
> ❦

The problem of Christians not living as disciples should isn't just in America.

were slaughtered, left me similarly confused. This area, which was at the heart of the East African revival, was in theory one of the most 'Christian' places on the planet at the time.

The problem of Christians not living as disciples should isn't just in America or in Africa: in my experience it is closer to home. My own personal observations, in local church life in England and in my ministry in the wider church, have underlined these deep concerns. I have known Christian leaders who have been living double lives over many years. They preach the word regularly, yet at the same time are regularly unfaithful to their wives. I also know of other Christians who love to speak of how they have not paid tax in situations where they clearly should have.

I have also been concerned about the tendency Christians have to divide from other Christians, often over quite inconsequential issues. Individuals separate from others; staying in the same church, meeting at the same communion table, but having no relationship with each other, sometimes for many years. I see this inclination towards division in churches that will have little or nothing to do with other churches because of minor doctrinal differences. These fractures in the Body, personal and collective, have sometimes remained unresolved for a long time, even though the Bible clearly teaches, 'Do not allow the sun to go down while you are still angry' (Eph. 4:26).

In my local church in the closing decades of the last century, evangelism was always *the* issue on our agenda. The great Billy Graham crusades would give

When Christians today reduce the gospel to forgiveness of sins, they are offering a one-sided, heretical message that is flatly unfaithful to the Jesus they worship as Lord and God. Only if we recover Jesus's gospel of the kingdom and allow its power to so transform our sinful selves that our Christian congregations (always imperfect to be sure) become visible holy signs of the dawning kingdom will we be faithful to Jesus. Only then will our evangelistic words recover integrity and power.

Ronald Sider, The Scandal of the Evangelical Conscience *(Grand Rapids: Baker Books, 2005)*

> ❧❧
>
> **How can we see those who come to faith grow to maturity in Christ?**
>
> ❧

us a boost, but in our local church we would go a long time, sometimes years, without seeing anyone come to faith in Christ. That is no longer the case. The issue today is: how can we see those who come to faith grow to maturity in Christ? Do those who are signing up to become Christians realise that they cannot do so without signing up to be whole life disciples of Jesus? This means taking on the 'world view' of Jesus so that gradually, through their walk with Jesus and their study of his teaching, they begin to view their lives and the world through his eyes. We cannot respond to the call of Jesus just to get peace of mind today and some kind of insurance guarantee about the future. The only response to the call of Jesus open to us is the response of submission to him as the Lord of our lives, a submission that can only be expressed in whole life discipleship.

In many parts of the world that I have the privilege to visit with my work with Operation Mobilisation, I find similar issues. Nations which just a generation ago were considered prime mission objectives have now become mission-sending nations. But many of the leaders of the churches in these nations are concerned that the growth they are witnessing may be wide but not deep.

> ❧❧
>
> **Much that passes for New Testament Christianity is little more than objective truth sweetened with song and made palatable by religious entertainment.**[3]
>
> *A. W. Tozer*

❧❦❧

In my youth I was once told by a well-meaning Sunday School teacher that it did not matter how I lived morally. If I was a Christian (defined as someone who had accepted Jesus Christ as Savior by performing a certain prayer), then I was eternally secure and could live any way I chose. Now this teacher, a godly person, was quick to add that living a morally bankrupt life was not God's will and would certainly bring my life into chaos . . . However, it is this teacher's initial idea that I want to challenge. I maintain that the implication (the possibility of a morally bankrupt life for a Christian without endangering eternal status) is both inconsistent with the gospel and with the way the New Testament describes the effects of salvation.[4]

Sam McKnight

❦

Amazing grace

This has all raised fundamental questions for me: questions about the gospel we are preaching, about the teaching in our churches and about our basic understanding of what it means to be Christian. But, thank God, I have also seen the other side: people totally transformed by the power of Christ. This transformation has not just affected their Sunday schedule, it has had an impact on their entire lives. I have seen families transformed and even communities, and the transformation has been deep and lasting.

> I have seen families transformed.

As I was writing this, I read the daily e-mail I receive from Chuck Colson, called BreakPoint. It records two stories of 'mind-boggling injustice and mind-bending mercy.' Here is a summary of one of those stories. Willie 'Pete' Williams, an African-American from Georgia, served more than two decades in prison for crimes he didn't commit. He was convicted in 1985 of aggravated sodomy, kidnapping and rape, and sentenced to forty-five years imprisonment. Williams always claimed his innocence and the Innocence Project took up his case. After investigations, they took the case back to court and Williams was found to be not guilty.

After singing a few lines of *Amazing Grace*, forty-four-year old Williams walked out of prison a free man and went home to eat a steak dinner with his family. A few days later, he appeared at a news conference, claiming he wasn't angry about spending half of his life behind bars. Instead he demonstrated mercy and forgiveness. 'Anybody can screw up,' he said. 'We're all human.' Williams attributes his remarkable ability to forgive to his conversion to Christ in prison. 'That's been my rock,' he said. His faith in Christ carried him through years of being labelled a sex offender and gave him hope that his innocence would one day come to light.

And why should it be me who writes this book? I have struggled for months with the answer. I have enjoyed running all my life, but I've never considered writing a book on running. However hard I try, I am not a great runner. I struggle to get under forty minutes over ten kilometres and to get under three hours for a marathon would take everything I've got and a little bit more. I suppose I've always thought that a book on running should be written by someone who gets closer to the two hour than the three hour mark over the marathon distance.

When it comes to discipleship I am definitely not a two-hour man! I've had everything going for me. My parents prayed that I would be a Christ-follower from the moment they knew I was on the way. They prayed daily and they modelled discipleship for me. I have had the privilege of being part of a church where scores of people pray for me regularly and again model the life for me. But I've been a struggler with

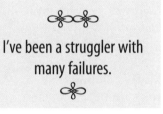

I've been a struggler with many failures.

many failures and I'm a struggler still. Yet as the years have passed, the desire has grown and, by God's grace, progress has been made. I can honestly say that I am not what I was. My desire for more is great. I believe God wants me to share some of these experiences with you, and perhaps a disciple who has struggled will have more to say to others who struggle than one who has not. That is my only defence for writing this book.

Questions

1. How can it be that there are those who believe they are Christians and yet quite clearly disobey the clear commands of God? How did we get into the position where people can live like this and still believe they are committed Christians?
2. If, as you have read this chapter, you have realised this is a description of you, what must you do now? Take a look at the church in Laodicea as described in Revelation 3:14–22, as you consider your answer.

Books

Ron Sider, *The Scandal of the Evangelical Conscience* (Grand Rapids: Baker books, 2005).

George Barna, *Boiling Point – It Only Takes One Degree* (Ventura, CA: Regal, 2001).

Part One

Principles

Chapter One

Born again

All over the world, we are witnessing people, like Pete Williams (see Introduction), totally transformed by the power of Christ. There is equally no doubt that we are also witnessing people who have an interest in Christ, some attachment to the Christian religion, but neither they or those who are familiar with their lives would describe their experiences as total transformation. Some of these people express concern for those whose lives have been totally transformed. 'Aren't they taking things a little too far? I am prepared to attend church and I will put my collection on the plate, the Christian Aid collector will always get a contribution when he comes to my door. But these people who talk about total transformation worry me, because some of them don't just talk it: they live it! They seem to give so much away, even more than a tenth of their income it appears in some cases. I don't think their golf handicap is ever going to get to down to single figures, because they seem so committed to their church and other Christian activities, and as for a weekend bolt hole, well, I think if they had one they would never get adequate use from it.'

We delude ourselves if we think that because we have made some decision we are done with it and forever secure in God's eyes. We delude ourselves if we think that we can lead immoral lives, shack up with partners who are not our spouses, defraud others of their money, take no action to alleviate social ills in our world, and live in constant tension with our children and family members – we delude ourselves … if we think we can live like this and pretend that we are at peace with God and enjoy his Son's justifying work.[5]

Sam McKnight

The most recent statistics in the UK inform us that 72% of the population here call themselves Christians, but for how many does that mean the total transformation of their lives? The parts of the

Are there different levels of Christian commitment at available to us?

church that are growing most rapidly in the world are those who could be described as either charismatic or evangelical, and many would be happy with both of those designations. But the findings from surveys such as that mentioned in the previous chapter lead to the question; to what degree is their experience leading to life transformation?

So are there different levels of Christian commitment available to us? When we sign up in response to the Christian challenge, can we join at different levels, depending on the price we are willing to pay? I fly a lot with my job and I am right now trying to decide at what level I should subscribe to a particular airline passenger association. The price I am willing to pay will determine the benefits I will receive. Is that how it is with the call of Christ?

However much that may appear to be the case, it is absolutely not the case. I firmly believe that we often get discipleship wrong at the beginning. To put it bluntly, we attempt to disciple those who are not Christians. They may have a respect for Jesus and some attachment to the Christian religion but, to use the language of Jesus, they have not been 'born of the Spirit' (Jn. 3:5). This, of course, is not the only reason people struggle with discipleship. For many, there has certainly been a genuine work of God in their lives and there is a desire to follow him, but they have never fully understood what is involved in following Jesus and take little account of the price that will need to be paid.

You must be born again

'No-one can see the kingdom of God unless he is born again' (Jn. 3:3). This was the challenge of Jesus to Nicodemus. Nicodemus was a religious man. His qualifications were impressive: he was a member of the Sanhedrin, a Pharisee and therefore someone who would be zealous for the law of God. Jesus called him 'Israel's teacher' (Jn. 3:10) and some suggest he might have been the most prominent religious teacher in the area at the time. He was familiar with Old Testament Scripture and was most probably trying to live out its principles. But Jesus was quite clear. Nicodemus needed something more if he was ever going to be right with God: so much more that the only way to describe it is as being 'born again.' These words could also be translated 'born from above.'

Jesus is referring to a supernatural experience, something Nicodemus could not do for himself. He is talking about a total and radical experience: not an alteration, but a total revolution; in fact regeneration, a totally new life. Though this is something God would do for Nicodemus in a moment, it would take him a lifetime to appreciate and respond to all that God was doing.

I was listening to an evangelistic presentation on a CD the day before I wrote these words. At the end of the presentation, the speaker said; 'All you need to do now is pray these words after me.' A simple prayer followed and the speaker then assured his listeners; 'If you said those words after me, you are now a Christian and all you need to do is find another Christian and tell them

Commenting on the teaching of the gospel writer, John, Liam Goligher writes

…Christian fellowship is with the Father and the Son, and … he will make it abundantly clear that nobody can enjoy a relationship with God without enjoying a relationship with Jesus (1 Jn. 2:23).

John starts with God. … He doesn't presume that Christian people will invariably have right thoughts of God. He says, 'This is the message we have heard from him (Jesus) and declare to you: God is light (1 Jn. 1:5). There you have the difference between liberal and biblical theology. Liberal theology always puts man in the centre. Biblical theology always puts God in the centre.

Liam Goligher, The Jesus Gospel –
Recovering the Lost Message
(Milton Keynes: Authentic, 2006)

what you have done.' There was absolutely no explanation of the radical nature of conversion and the whole life impact that must follow; no understanding conveyed to those present that this meant total submission to Jesus as the Lord of their lives. I believe the speaker, though sincere, was presenting a totally inadequate picture of what it means to become a Christian. I was also concerned that, as the hearers gradually heard of the demands of discipleship, they might even believe they had been deceived.

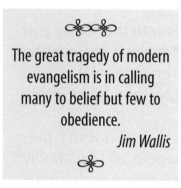

The great tragedy of modern evangelism is in calling many to belief but few to obedience.

Jim Wallis

When Jesus speaks of being 'born again' he is referring to the work of God in our lives whereby we receive his divine nature. We receive the Lord Jesus Christ into our lives, his Spirit takes residence within us and our bodies become the temple in which he lives. This must lead to whole life transformation and whole life discipleship, as we submit to his rule and authority. This will transform us as much on Monday morning in our place of work as on Sunday morning in our place of worship. It will transform us as much when we are supporting our favourite football team as it does when we are alone at home with our spouse or our parents.

This must lead to whole life transformation.

On one occasion Jesus met someone who was impressed by him, and who greeted him with the words 'Good teacher' (Mk. 10:17). This man was quite an impressive person himself, and is sometimes referred to in Bible headings as the rich young ruler. When Jesus quoted five of the Ten Commandments to him, he replied 'All these I have kept since I was a boy.' He had clearly done well in life; he had made some serious money (v22). But he knew that this life in which he had done so well was not all there was. He was concerned about life after death and wanted to be sure all would be well with him for the future. Had he seen that Jesus would be the key to his well being in eternity? Was he considering following Jesus as his disciple? Jesus placed a challenge before him, knowing his soft spot exactly. 'One thing you lack . . . Go, sell everything you have and give to the poor, and you will have treasure in heaven. Then come, follow me' (v21).

No other call

There are no half measures with Jesus; the call to follow transforms every area of our lives and there is no other call. There are no differing levels of subscription when you join his kingdom. Although Jesus made it very clear that we must fully consider the cost before committing our lives to follow him, the whole idea that we can calmly consider the pros and cons with a take it or leave it attitude is to misunderstand. This is the Lord of Heaven and earth calling us to follow him. We must realise this is going to cost everything but it is going to gain us everything. The one question is: are we ready to follow, giving him everything, making him the Lord of our lives? There is

When Christ calls a man, he bids him come and die.
Dietrich Bonhoeffer[6]

no other question to answer because nothing else is on offer.

The apostle Paul also stresses the totally radical nature of conversion and discipleship: 'If anyone is in Christ, he is a new creation; the old has gone, the new has come!' (2 Cor. 5:17). This had been Paul's own experience. From the moment he realised that Christ had defeated death and had died for him, his whole worldview was changed. Paul's view of himself, of others and of Christ was transformed. Things he once considered to be of supreme value, he now considered rubbish. The only thing he now considered to be truly important is how he stood before God.

> It is a lifelong discovery and a lifelong struggle.

Eugene Peterson paraphrases Paul's words 'Because of this decision we don't evaluate people by what they have or how they look. We looked at the Messiah that way once and got it all wrong, as you know' (2 Cor. 5:16 The Message). This transformed mind was not a once-for-all transformation, but the beginning of a lifelong adventure. It is a lifelong discovery and a lifelong struggle. The rest of the book will seek to explain this adventure and help with these struggles.

Saved, converted or committed?

When I was a child, preachers used to talk about people being *saved*. As time passed the language changed and preachers spoke of people being *converted*. Then it changed again and people were asked to make a *commitment* or a *profession*. Saved: that is something done for you;

an act of God on your behalf. It sounds both urgent and radical. Converted: that is something you can do for yourself but it still sounds radical. But to make a commitment, that sounds like something you or I do for ourselves. It also sounds as though it could be one commitment you choose to make among many.

Becoming a Christian is not making a new start in life; it is receiving a new life to start with.

John Blanchard

I am not advocating the use of outdated language but I am concerned that we appreciate and proclaim that conversion is an act of God. It is a new birth; a person is transformed to become part of a new creation. A kingdom is entered and total submission to the King of Kings must now be our experience. This submission is a daily struggle as the flesh lusts against the Spirit and the Spirit wars against the flesh.

What do people believe they are being asked to sign up for when they are given the challenge to follow Christ? Do they imagine it is to do with cleaning up their lifestyles, joining a new club, securing their future? It is vital that from the very beginning they understand this is new birth and no stone of their lives can remain unturned. If we get it wrong here, we will never get discipleship right.

So can I encourage you to go back to the beginning; that day or that period when you came face to face with Jesus Christ and realised who he was? It is possible you did not

If we get it wrong here, we will never get discipleship right.

understand the fullness of the privilege, challenge or cost of following him because that was not explained to you. Don't worry! He still stands and he still calls and the opportunity is always open to us to start afresh. Your reading of this book may be part of that new beginning.

Questions

1. When you became a Christian, what did you sign up to? A Saviour who would forgive your sins and take your worries away? Or a Lord who would rule your life?
2. 'All you need to be converted is to believe in Jesus Christ and to invite him into your life.' Why is that statement insufficient? Read James 3:14–26 as you reflect on this question.

Further study – What does Jesus expect of those who follow him? Read Luke 14:25–33 and the interview between Jesus and Nicodemus in John 3:1–21.

Books

Jonathan Aitken, *Pride and Perjury* (London: Continuum, 2003).

Chuck Colson, *Born Again* (London: Hodder & Stoughton, 2005).

Rodney Combs, *Bonhoeffer's the Cost of Discipleship* (Shepherd's Notes Christian Classics, B&H Publishing Group, 1999).

Richard Foster, *Celebration of Discipline* (London: Hodder & Stoughton, 1998).

Vaughan Roberts, *Distinctives* (Milton Keynes: Authentic, 2000).

Dominic Smart, *When We Get it Wrong* (Milton Keynes: Authentic, 2001).

David Watson, *Discipleship* (London: Hodder & Stoughton, 1983).

Dallas Willard, *The Spirit of the Disciplines – Understanding How God Changes Lives* (Harper SanFrancisco, 1991).

For evangelistic courses and the basics of the faith, see the following

alpha.org
www.christianityexplored.com.

Other resources that can be used in small groups include

Rico Tice and Barry Cooper, *Christianity Explored* (Milton Keynes: Authentic, 2002) – there are many books and resources available in this series.

Peter Meadows and Joseph Steinberg, *The Book of Y* (Milton Keynes: Authentic, 2007).

Chapter Two

What is a disciple?

So what is a disciple? It is not only Christians who talk about disciples. We hear of the disciples of eastern mystics, business gurus or even fashion designers. In these cases, being a disciple means following the ideas, the teachings of your guru. The Oxford dictionary definition of discipleship also gives this idea: 'one who takes another as his teacher and model.'

> ❦
> **Their call to discipleship was a call to be with Jesus.**
> ❦

When Jesus spoke of discipleship he meant all of that, but so much more. When we look at the first disciples of Jesus, we see that their call to discipleship was a call to be with Jesus.

As Jesus was walking beside the Sea of Galilee, he saw two brothers, Simon called Peter and his brother Andrew. They were casting a net into the lake, for they were fishermen. "Come, follow me," Jesus said, "and I will make you fishers of men." At once they left their nets and followed him (Mt. 4:18–20).

> As he walked along, he saw Levi son of Alphaeus sitting at the tax collector's booth. "Follow me," Jesus told him, and Levi got up and followed him (Mk. 2:14).

Jesus' call to discipleship is not an invitation to participate in a programme or even to share in a cause but to be with a Person, so that he can make us into the people he wants us to be. The call to discipleship is the call to relationship, a relationship that will gradually make us all that God intended us to be. We were

The call to discipleship is the call to relationship.

made for relationship with God, but sin put distance between our Father and us. Jesus has come from the Father and, at great cost, has opened the door to relationship again. Discipleship is the outworking of that restored relationship.

Disciples of business or fashion gurus can follow their ideas without any relationship with the gurus themselves. It can never be that way for disciples of Jesus; a personal, daily relationship with Jesus is at the very heart of discipleship. It is so vital that, at this point, we understand Christian discipleship is not just following teaching, keeping a set of rules or practising particular techniques; it is walking through life with a Friend.

The ordinary Christian life

As we have already seen, the impression is sometimes given that a life of discipleship is the Premier Division of the Christian life. Just as there are other divisions in which your football team can play, so there are other

Who teaches you? Whose disciple are you? Honestly. One thing is sure: You are somebody's disciple. You learned how to live from somebody else. There are no exceptions to this rule, for human beings are just the kind of creatures that have to learn and keep learning from others how to live. . . Today, especially in Western cultures, we prefer to think that we are 'our own person'. . . . Such individualism is part of the legacy that makes us 'modern'. But we certainly did not come by that individualistic posture through our own individual and independent insight into ultimate truth. . . It is one of the major transitions of life to recognise who has taught us, mastered us, and then evaluate the results in us of their teaching.

Dallas Willard, The Divine Conspiracy,
(London: HarperCollins, 1998)

leagues of Christian living. But no: the life of discipleship is not the special life. It is not the *extraordinary* Christian life; it is the *ordinary* Christian life. It is the life every Christian should be living. It is life as God intended it to be; a life lost by our sin but with the possibility of its restoration, bought at great cost.

Discipleship is a call to a relationship of the highest priority. Simon, Andrew and Levi all had to make immediate and significant sacrifices in order to give this relationship what it would require. Jesus met two men who said they wanted to follow him and one whom he challenged to follow him (Lk. 9:57–62). It immediately became clear that they were not ready to give this relationship the priority that it demanded. They wanted to follow him but only if the conditions were right. They would follow on their terms, if it suited their circumstances.

The disciples of business gurus follow their teachings and methods: the disciples of Jesus have to have a personal allegiance to Jesus. The call to discipleship is a call to self-denial. Jesus made this quite remarkable statement: 'If anyone would come after me, he must deny himself and take up his cross and fol-

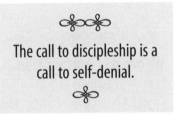

The call to discipleship is a call to self-denial.

low me' (Mk. 8:34). Who but the Son of God could ever give such a call?

The Son of God invites us to a relationship with him. The simple command to those early disciples was 'Follow me. I am on a journey and I want you to walk with me.' It was a journey that would call for the ultimate in self-denial, because this journey led to the cross. But thank God that was not the final destination. I've known for years that that this relationship must be my priority but I have consistently failed to give the time that is required to develop it. Other things, sometimes religious things, have got in the way.

In many ways this relationship is similar to others. It has the normal stuff of relationships: encouragements and discouragements, progress and regress, rewards and discipline. The disciples of the era of Jesus would spend time with their master, often actually moving in and living with him. If they didn't do that, they certainly spent hours every day watching, listening, discussing. Gradually they took on board the mind of the teacher. They began to think as he thought, viewing life the way their teacher saw it. They found themselves gradually reacting to the circumstances of life in the way their teacher did. To use more modern language, their worldview became that of their teacher.

This is the way disciples of Jesus are made today. As we spend time with him, time in his word, time with other disciples in community, we begin to embrace Jesus' worldview. This takes time: it is actually a lifelong course. But the impact is absolutely radical. Anyone who reads the New Testament can see that the way Jesus saw the world, the priorities and ambitions of his life, were utterly counter-cultural. In fact, his life was so radically different that it became utterly unacceptable and crucifixion was the result. Before we go any further with this journey, we need to ask 'Are we ready for a lifelong learning course and to pay the price for living the radically different life that Jesus calls us to?'

> We begin to embrace Jesus' worldview.

The practice of his presence

Never forget that we are talking about a relationship, not a system or programme to follow. There is no set of challenges that we must meet in order to qualify. Jesus, the Son of God, wants us to walk through life with him. What does that mean for me today? Practically, it means what might be called the practice of his presence. One thing which has become very real to me is the experience of constant conversation with Jesus.

It is amazing how many discipleship challenges have been placed before me over the years. These have often been presented as 'must do' things, in order to be a true disciple. I have been told I must have a quiet time every day. I must read the Bible through every year. I must spend a minimum of an hour in prayer every day. I must speak to at least one person about Jesus every day, and the list continues. The list of things I must not do in order to be a true disciple is even longer! Many of these things I have found to be helpful disciplines. Some, I confess, I have found to be helpful disciplines for a time, and then they have become a burden, a lifeless routine. But this one thing has become more and more real: the experience of sharing everything with the Lord Jesus and asking for his help and wisdom in the various situations faced each day. I often rush into things and have to stop myself and quite deliberately pause and recognise his presence.

Gradually, though sadly still inconsistently, I believe I am growing in the experience of seeing life,

> A disciple is a person who learns to live the life his teacher lives.
>
> *Juan Carlos Ortiz*

and seeing my life, through the eyes of Jesus. This has an ever-growing impact on my decision-making. Things that once were of great importance in that process are now far less important or even no longer important. I believe the more I see through the eyes of Jesus, the more his glory rather than my reputation influences my decisions and the more the eternal rather than the present consequence of those decisions becomes the controlling factor.

A love relationship

The discipleship relationship is, at its heart, a love relationship. Disciples of Jesus are people who love Jesus and want to be with him. They love him because of who he is, what he has done, and what he continues to do for them on a daily basis.

Disciples of Jesus are people who love Jesus.

Here we have reached a vital point in this book. I read some books on discipleship and after reading them, I don't want to be a disciple. It all sounds so heavy and demanding: true disciples seem to be people of utterly heroic self-denial. In fact, though, the moment we realise who Jesus is and what he has done for us, total commitment to him is the only life that makes any sense.

When I fell in love with the lady who is now my wife, I often missed the last bus home from her house. It was a long walk home. But as I made that walk, was I thinking how hard this was? Did I spend my time reflecting on the self-denial involved in developing this relationship? It never crossed my mind. Paying a price for the relationship was a joy, the very opposite of a heavy burden. Thirty-five years later, I can testify it is still a joy. If ever I am away preaching and am anywhere within

Love is the root; obedience is the fruit.

Matthew Henry

reach of getting home that night, I will always make the effort. But it doesn't seem like an effort. True disciples of Jesus are likely to be the most joyful, contented people you will ever meet.

We express our love to our spouses in a variety of ways. An important expression of love for me is to do things for Win. I love to serve her. Doing so is no hardship: it brings me great joy and I hope it does the same for her. In the same way, the service of Jesus is no hardship. There are hard times, many disappointments, but this is privilege. Service gets hard when my motives get messed up: when I am actually serving myself instead of Jesus; when I am looking for advantage for myself, promoting myself. Then the apparent service of Jesus can become competitive and relational tensions soon arise.

I like to start every day with these words; 'O Lord open my lips and my mouth shall proclaim your praise. Glory to the Father and to the Son and to the Holy Spirit. As it was in the beginning, is now and ever shall be: Amen.'

And I am not even an Anglican! But it really helps me to get my focus right for the day. This is

The question is still the same: Do you love Jesus? Affection is the answer to apathy.

Vance Havner

> Discipleship is more than getting to know what the teacher knows. It is getting to be what he is.
>
> *Juan Carlos Ortiz*

not about me. It is not about love for me. It is not about my comfort, my success, and my safety. I am his servant. He has bought me by paying the ultimate price. To love him and serve him is not heroic; it is the normal response of a person who understands more and more who Jesus is and appreciates more and more what he has done.

From time to time Win will sensitively let me know that while she appreciates the acts of service, she likes to hear me tell her that I love her. The occasional bunch of flowers is definitely appreciated. I think my personality finds it a lot easier to serve than to speak! I sometimes find myself a little envious of those who can express their emotions more freely than I in a worship service. We need to appreciate that God has made us different and learn to celebrate those differences. But I also need to be careful that I don't make that an excuse. God also longs to hear my words of love and worship. This has been a constant struggle in my desire to be a true disciple. *Activity* for God comes so much more easily than *adoration* of him. This is not to say that our activity is not an expression of our adoration but I know God loves to

> God loves to hear the expression of my heart in words.

hear the expression of my heart in words as well as works. 'Through Jesus, therefore, let us continually offer to God a sacrifice of praise – the fruit of lips that confess his name (Heb. 13:15).

Discipleship once appeared to me to be more about what I did than who I was. I was born into a wonderful Christian home and taken to church from nine months before I was born. As a young man, I went to all the services at the church that I could and saw that I got high marks from the leaders of the church for my attendance record. In my early teens, I came into contact with Operation Mobilisation. It was an incredibly active organisation. At that time giving out Christian literature everywhere you went was the order of the day, so I bought into that. Long prayer meetings were also very popular, so that became part of my life as well. Then I was given a book *Power through prayer*. It contained many stories of men and women who rose incredibly early in the day to pray. So who started to rise at 4am? I woke quite often on my knees, slumped into the arm-chair, about six!

A son, not a slave

When I was sixteen, God used these words to transform my life; 'So you are no longer a slave, but a son; and since you are a son, God has made you also an heir' (Gal. 4:7). I realised that I had become an evangelical slave. In order to please my Master, I felt I had to do things and as long as I

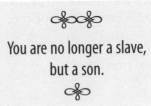

You are no longer a slave, but a son.

did those things faithfully, he would be pleased. The transformation, of course, was the realisation that I was a son, not a slave. My Master was also my Father and he was pleased with me, indeed delighted with me, because I was his son. I still continued to do many of the things that I had been doing. The change was in the motivation. No longer was I doing these things in order to please, but out of gratitude and love for the One who had already done everything for me. It was a totally life-transforming lesson for me.

In Luke 14:25 large crowds are travelling with Jesus. Every preacher loves a crowd and yet it seems to me that Jesus is concerned. 'Do these people really understand me? Do they appreciate in any way what I really stand for and what will be involved in following me?' In the verses that follow, Jesus places before them in the clearest terms the conditions of true discipleship. Where does

Every other love relationship must be subordinate to your love for me.

Jesus begin? 'If anyone comes to me and does not hate his father and mother, his wife and children, his brothers and sisters – yes, even his own life – he cannot be my disciple' (Lk. 14:26). Jesus is speaking about the deepest love relationships of our lives and yet he says; 'If you are to follow me, I must be the number one love relationship of your life. Every other love relationship must be subordinate to your love for me.'

Questions

1. How would you describe yourself – a child of God, a servant of God, a colleague of God, or a slave of God?
2. To be a disciple is to be with Jesus. What does being with Jesus mean to you?

Books

Oswald Chambers, *My Utmost for His Highest*.

J.I. Packer, *Knowing God* (London: Hodder & Stoughton, 2005).

Adrian Plass, *Jesus, Safe, Tender, Extreme* (Grand Rapids: Zondervan, 2006).

John Stott, *The Incomparable Christ* (Leicester: IVP, 2001).

A.W. Tozer, *The Knowledge of the Holy* (Milton Keynes: Authentic Classics, 2005).

Philip Yancey, *The Jesus I Never Knew* (Grand Rapids: Zondervan, 1998).

Chapter Three

The demands of discipleship

Imagine for a moment that you are waking up on the morning of the last day of your life. Your execution time has already been fixed for later in the day. All the plans that you had mapped out, the unfulfilled desires, the unachieved goals: there is no way now these can ever be realised. It is the end.

Jesus could not have been clearer. 'Anyone who does not carry his cross and follow me cannot be my disc-iple' (Lk. 14:27). We cannot receive new life from him unless there is death to the old life. The previous way we used to live, the ambi-tions, the priorities, the motivations by which we lived, must come to an end. It is a whole new life we are entering. I fear that for many today, being a Christian is seen as a pleasant extra experience we add to our already pleasant lives. But Jesus said following him involves cross bearing.

> It is a whole new life we are entering.

This is how the Christian life must begin. There must be repentance from sin, a turning away from sin in our lives and a turning in faith towards the Lord Jesus Christ. This turning away from sin means a decisive decision to totally reject all known evil in our lives. The next few paragraphs may take extra concentration to understand but if we can grasp the truths contained in them it will be totally transforming, so please work with me.

In 2 Corinthians 5:14, Paul argues that 'one died for all, and therefore all died.' When Christ died 'for all' he paid the 'wages of sin': not his own, as he was sinless, but yours and mine. Thank God, Christ paid the penalty for sin once and for all. God raised his Son from the dead and, in that action, God proclaimed his absolute satisfaction with the work that Jesus had done. Through our identification with Christ in his death – 'we died with Christ' (Rom. 6:8), our sins have been forever dealt with by the work of Christ. The person that I used to be, my 'old self' (Rom. 6:6), died with Christ. But Scripture is very clear and my experience certainly supports this, that there are still many things in my life that need to be put to death every day. So what died when I died with Christ?

We know only too well that it is not our old nature, our flesh, that has died. We have 'died to sin' in the sense that the penalty of our sin has been forever and fully paid: the person we used to be has been crucified with Christ. This is what it means to be born again. The person that I used to be died with Christ, but I was also raised with Christ, raised a new person.

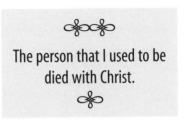

The person that I used to be died with Christ.

In this new person, sin no longer reigns, Jesus is Lord. When my old nature seeks to reassert its rule in my life, I must

> ❦
>
> **They that deny themselves for Christ shall enjoy themselves in Christ.**
>
> *J.M. Mason*
>
> ❦

remember the new reality. We must 'count' ourselves 'dead to sin but alive to God in Christ Jesus' (Rom. 6:11). There has been a death to sin and now there must be death to self. Thank God for the promise of his Holy Spirit, for without him we would never have come to Christ and found new life. Without him we could never know victory in this ongoing battle with self.

In our church we practise baptism by immersion and I can never witness a baptism without getting emotional. What a visual statement it is: the image of the end, the death and burial of the old life as the candidate goes under the water; then the rising from the water, depicting the new birth. A whole new life has begun, lived in the power of the Holy Spirit, a life where sin no longer reigns.

So even though we are made new in Christ, we must continue to carry our cross. Continual repentance and a constant turning to Christ for forgiveness and strength

> ❦
>
> **We must continue to carry our cross.**
>
> ❦

become the pattern of our lives. We learn to build into our lives habits which keep us looking to Christ, relying on his Spirit's power and rejecting the constant pull of the flesh towards evil.

John Stott writes 'The Christian life continues where it begins at the foot of the cross of Jesus. The cross is not an elementary stage, which we later grow out of. We never

The very purpose of Christ's coming to earth, the New Testament declares, was to create a holy community: Christ "gave himself for us to redeem us from all wickedness and to *purify for himself a people* that are his very own, eager to do what is good" (Titus 2:14, italics mine). St Paul also insists that Christ came precisely to create a holy church: "Christ loved the church and gave himself up for her to make her holy, cleansing her by the washing with water through the word, and to present her to himself as a radiant church, without stain or wrinkle or any other blemish, but holy and blameless" (Eph. 5:25–27).

Ronald Sider, The Scandal of the Evangelical Conscience *(Grand Rapids: Baker Books, 2005)* graduate from the school of Calvary. And the Lord's Supper continuously brings us back to it.'[7] This is for me another vital part of life in my local church. The experience of regularly breaking bread and drinking wine with my brothers and sisters reminds me of so many things. It reminds me of how much I am loved and valued, and that this relationship is a relationship of love. It reminds me that just as Jesus died for my sin, and the person that I used to be died with him, I must die daily to self, by the power of the Spirit. It reminds me that Jesus did not stay on the cross: he rose and he lives today, in me, by his gracious powerful Spirit.

We can see this in the life of Peter, who needed to learn to die daily to his own ambitions and desires (Mt. 16:21–23). With Jesus nearing the end of his time with his disciples, he begins to explain to them 'that he must go to Jerusalem and suffer many things at the hands of the elders, chief priests and teachers of the law, and that he must be killed and on the third day be raised to life.' Peter's response is immediate and it's a rebuke to Jesus. 'Never, Lord! This shall never happen to you!' Peter responds like this because he does 'not have in mind the things of God, but the things of men.'

Peter may be a new man but there is work still to do. He does not yet see things from God's perspective. The transformation will continue, as we know from the Acts of the Apostles and from the letters he wrote, but the process is not yet complete. He wants to protect Jesus and this is an admirable motive. But for Jesus self-protection is not the issue, only the will of his Father is of consequence. We see this most clearly in the

> ❈
> **Jesus' will and his life were totally abandoned to his Father.**
> ❈

garden of Gethsemane. 'My Father, if it is not possible for this cup to be taken away unless I drink it, may your will be done' (Mt. 26:42). Jesus' will and his life were totally abandoned to his Father and to his Father's purposes.

Jesus takes the opportunity from the conversation

God creates out of nothing. Therefore until a man is nothing, God can make nothing out of him.
Martin Luther

with Peter to show the nature of true discipleship. 'If anyone would come after me, he must deny himself and take up his cross and follow me. For whoever wants to save his life will lose it, but whoever loses his life for me will find it' (Mt. 22:24,25). Discipleship demands the abandonment of self-preservation. To follow Jesus, we must get to that point where we understand doing the will of God is the important issue, not what happens to us. Whether I am married or single is a huge issue but it is not *the* issue. Whether I have children or don't can be equally huge. Whether I am healthy or unwell is a massive issue but it is not *the* issue. Whether I am wealthy or poor is an issue and will certainly impact my life, but it's not *the* issue. Whether God asks me to live in Birmingham or Bangladesh will be of great significance but it's not *the* issue.

Does God owe me?

There was a forty-eight hour period when I was afraid that I might lose one

Discipleship demands the abandonment of self-preservation.

of my sons, Tim. I spent most of those hours in the hospital room where he was recovering from an operation. There were complications in the recovery process and something was going on in his body that, for about thirty-six hours, the medical team could not understand. It was a period of considerable uncertainty and confusion for Win and myself, though much more for Tim: a traumatic time.

I will never forget the wrestling with God. Could I entrust my son to my Father's will? Could I, at this critical moment, say 'Thy will be done on earth as it is in heaven'? Or was that just something I repeated in a prayer? Did I only want his will for my life when it suited how I thought life should go? I was not able just to hand my son over. I fought, I wept, I complained bitterly. 'Have I not sought to serve you as faithfully as I could? Have there not been sacrifices I have made for you?' I was slipping into entitlement thinking. Didn't God owe me?

Have I not sought to serve you as faithfully as I could?

I don't remember all the details of those hours, but I am sure that was one of the many occasions, in connection with my family, that Abraham came to my mind. The impact of my ministry lifestyle on my family has been one of the big issues of my discipleship. As I share elsewhere in this book, I believe I have failed and asked too much of them at times. But in that hospital room, and many times as I have been waving goodbye at the start of another journey, the image has come to my mind of Abraham, called by God to leave everything in his home city of Ur of the Chaldees, starting out without even knowing where he was heading. Then, later, God tells him to sacrifice the son on whom all his hopes for the future seem to rest. Did I have the faith of Abraham that would release in me the obedience of Abraham?

It was a long battle in that hospital room to get to that point. When I finally got there, within a short time the problem was identified and the crisis quickly over. I am very conscious in writing this that others have got to that point possibly far quicker than I did but have not been blessed with a similar outcome. I can only trust that my resolve would have remained unchanged if the outcome had been different.

A new drumbeat

I learned that we will never get to this point of total abandonment to the will of the Father, regardless of what that means, without repentance; that initial and decisive rejection of evil and the domination of the flesh, and the continual dying to self that must follow. In fact, says Jesus, we must lose our lives. As we have seen, our goals, ambitions and motives must die. Living life in our own strength must cease. As we rise

We must lose our lives.

from the water in baptism, we are saying to the Lord, 'My life is finished, the person that used to be is no more. I have received your resurrection life, the life of your Spirit and from now on I march to your drumbeat, not my own.'

It all sounds so sacrificial and, if death is involved, then there is sacrifice. But we must never forget this totally liberating statement from Jesus; 'Whoever loses his life for me will find it' (Mt. 16:25). It is our willingness to die that opens the door to life. Here is the great lie of our enemy, that we will have to give up so much. People refuse to come to Christ, saying they could never make such sacrifices. And we lie to them if we minimize what must be given up. But the reality is we are never more alive than when we die to self: for we have been 'crucified with Christ . . . I no longer live but Christ lives in me' (Gal. 2:20). We are never more fully human than when we die. We do not begin to live as our Creator intended us to live until we die.

Questions

1. 'The doctrine of death to self will lead to the obliteration of our personalities.' Is this a true statement and, if not, explain how we can die to self and still be ourselves.
2. Think back over the last twenty-four hours: can you recall making any decisions where you chose to die to self and live for Christ? Do you regret any of those decisions?

Books

Elisabeth Elliott, *The Shadow of the Almighty* (Milton Keynes: Authentic Media, 1988).

Michael Griffiths, *Take My Life* (Carlisle: STL, 1984).

David Watson, *You Are My God* (London: Hodder & Stoughton, 1983).

John White, *The Fight* (Leicester: IVP, 2002).

Chapter Four

Death to self – living in the light of eternity

Imagine for a moment that you are building up a business, going through difficult times, and yet you know the ultimate result of your labours, even as you are at work. Imagine you are a general, leading your troops into the war zone, and even before hostilities begin, you know the final result of the battle. In the last chapter we saw that if we are to live the life of

The end is not death.

discipleship, we must be constantly looking back to the cross and to our dying with Christ there. But we also must constantly be looking forward to the end of our lives of discipleship, and we know the end is not death.

In Operation Mobilisation, we have two ships. I have only managed a couple of voyages over the years and I like to hang over the deck railings as we set sail. The huge ropes are loosened from their moorings and the ship moves away. As it leaves dock, preparations are already being made for the next port of call. The captain knows where he is taking the ship. When Paul uses the word departure to describe his own death (2 Tim. 4:6), that is the image he has in mind. He is leaving one shore but the Captain is in control and will take him safely to the next.

This absolute confidence of knowing what happens at death and at the end of time should be a major influence on our lives of discipleship. If we are going to get discipleship right we must live our lives and make our choices and decisions, constantly looking back to the cross and forward to eternity. An important biblical emphasis is that we are pilgrims; we are walking through this world, walking towards our eternal hope.

Hebrews 11 records the exploits of some remarkable men and women of faith. A key to their lives of faith is that 'they admitted they were aliens and strangers on earth' (Heb. 11:13). This did not stop them making a contribution to life on this earth, their contribution was immense, but as they worked 'they were longing for a better country – a heavenly one' (Heb. 11:16).

Temporary residents

Christ's disciples realise they are only temporary residents here. Our permanent home is being prepared for us (Jn. 14:2–3), so we refuse to settle down permanently. I remember a missionary family who had responded to the call of God to Papua New Guinea. It would be a few months, however, before they would leave, and it was very interesting to watch them during those months. They knew that where they were living was far from permanent

> **Our permanent home is being prepared for us.**

I do not know if Jim had any premonition that God was going to take him up on all he had promised Him – going to answer literally his prayer of April 18, 1948: 'Father, take my life, yea, my blood if Thou wilt, and consume it with Thine enveloping fire. I would not save it for it is not mine to save. Have it, Lord, have it all. Pour out my life as an oblation for the world.'

Elisabeth Elliot,
The Shadow of the Almighty
(Milton Keynes: Authentic Classics, 2005)

and all their choices were made with that in mind. As they considered buying things, they were constantly asking themselves: 'Can I take this with me? If I buy many of these, are they going to be wasted?'

The more we realise that we are only temporary residents here and dwell on that fact, the more we will differ from those around us, who live their lives only for today. While Christ calls us to live in the world, living with eternity in view will mean we are always going to find there will be a measure of isolation and dislocation from those around us. They will find some of our choices and decisions strange, and may even be offended by them.

Jesus gives a clear choice: we can live for this earth or we can live for heaven (Mt. 6:19–21). The individual who is really in trouble is the one who cannot make up their mind. The person whose 'treasure' is this world has made up their mind, and is clear where they are going, what they are aiming for, but so many try to straddle the fence. They know where their treasure should be but they just cannot make that ultimate decision and finally abandon living for the here and now.

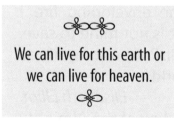

We can live for this earth or we can live for heaven.

The temporary Christian resident living with eternity in view realises that all they really need is enough to keep themselves and their families alive. Our generous God often gives far more than that, and when he does, we receive it gratefully from his generous hand. But the temporary resident is not going to pursue 'the more' nor are they going to tire themselves out chasing the treasures of this earth, leaving no time for investment in eternity. Many Christians have chosen a standard of living which can only be supported by an utterly hectic lifestyle. They do not have time for the things they know should have priority. I appreciate that many Christians these days have

The question is: where is our treasure?

to work very hard just to make ends meet. However, other Christians I know choose a higher style of living which can only be supported by an utterly exhausting working life. The question is: where is our treasure?

Making sense of life

Paul is clear in his correspondence with the Corinthians that the way he is living makes no sense whatsoever if there is no certain and secure eternal future. First he challenges their mysterious practice of baptism for the dead. I think we have to say we are unsure of exactly what Paul is referring to here, but there is no difficulty with his logic. 'If the dead are not raised at all, why are people baptized for them?' (1 Cor. 15:29). It just doesn't make sense. It is just the same with Paul's life, he continues; 'And as for us, why do we endanger ourselves every hour?' (v30). Taking risks and deciding on life-threatening choices for the cause of Christ makes no sense if this life is all there is, but every sense if you are living life with the certainty of a glorious future.

Paul really seemed to have grasped the secret of living in this way. As he writes his first letter to the Thessalonians, he has been facing all manner of difficulties and criticisms. How does he keep going? He writes; 'We are not trying to please men but God, who tests our hearts' (1 Thess. 2:4). He understood that he lived his life in the presence of God and to God he must one day answer. When, at the end of his life, Paul is challenging Timothy to keep going in the ministry, there is the same emphasis; 'In the presence of God and of Christ Jesus, who will judge the living and the dead, and in view of his appearing and his kingdom, I give you this charge' (2 Tim. 4:1). He lived his life confident that one day he would stand before God, that his death would not be the end but a new beginning, and this had a fundamental impact on the daily decisions of his life. In another context he wrote; 'If only for this life we have hope in Christ, we are to be pitied more than all men' (1 Cor. 15:19). His life, his decisions, his risk-taking made no sense if his hope in Christ was only for this life.

The watchword of the pioneers of the modern missionary movement was 'Let's bring back the King.' Fundamental to their life choices, leading to the most amazing advances of the mission's movement, at enormous human cost, was the conviction of the King's triumphant return. The pioneer missionaries who went

Let's bring back the King.

inland in Africa did not expect a long life; in fact some took their coffins with them. Decisions such as these can only be understood in the light of their conviction that death was not the end but that their work would be instrumental in bringing back the King and his reign in all its fullness.

Peter is also clear that there are ethical and motivational implications if this is our hope. He knew it wouldn't be long before the cynics were raising their voices. 'They will say, "Where is this 'coming' he promised? Ever since our fathers died, everything goes on as it has since the beginning of creation"' (2 Pet. 3:4). They deliberately forgot the flood in the days of Noah (2 Pet. 3:5,6). God had intervened in judgment before and one day will again. This coming judgment is a terrifying prospect for those who don't know Christ. It is at the same time both a comforting and a hugely motivating prospect for those who do. 'But in keeping with his promise we are looking forward to a new heaven and a new earth, the home of righteousness' (2 Pet. 3 :13).

The more I travel and the more I see of the tragedies and injustices in this world, the more I look forward to this future home of righteousness. I regularly take comfort and find motivation in the truth that there will be no HIV/AIDS there, no death, no pain, no oppression of the weak by the strong or the poor by the rich. Peter shows we can work to bring that day to pass, 'speed its coming' (2 Pet. 3:12). This will not only be accomplished by what we do but also by what we

You ought to live holy and godly lives.

are. Peter's challenge is; if you believe these things, 'what kind of people ought you to be?' (2 Pet. 3:11). His answer; 'You ought to live holy and godly lives.'

I need people to whom I am accountable on a regular basis. I know that the brothers I meet with are going to ask me direct questions, and though I hope the thought of being asked those questions is not the primary motivation for what I do and refuse to do, it is an added motivation. My final and true accountability, however, will be to the Lord himself, and Peter is clear this is a healthy motivation for holy living. The Christian who lives the life of true discipleship will constantly be looking back to the cross, reminded of how much they are loved, and of their death with Christ there. They will be

There was a day when I died to George Muller; his opinions and preferences, taste and will; died to the world, its approval or censure, died to the approval or blame even of brothers or friends, and since then I have striven only to show myself approved unto God.

George Muller

constantly looking to the future, an absolutely certain future, which will be both a great motivation and comfort.

Every day in the light of that day

Martin Luther seemed to have learned the secret of living like this. He said; 'There are only two days in my diary, today and that day.' That is the challenge of the disciple: to live every day in the light of that final day. One man, when asked what he would do if he knew Christ would return tomorrow, answered that he would continue with his programme as planned! He had learned this lesson of living in the light of eternity, 'every day in the light of that day.'

It is taking me much longer to get to that point. I had a great time at school, though my concentration was on sports rather than education. I never went to university and for years I struggled with that, particularly when I was in the company of those who were a lot more educated than I was. I found myself constantly trying to prove myself, even pretending that I knew things that I didn't, so that I would not be seen as a total idiot! The whole focus of my life was wrong. I needed two things. I needed to look back to the cross and realise my total acceptance by Christ, not on the basis of performance but through my position as a son. I needed to look forward to the last day: not living driven by what I imagined were the expectations of others but by the understanding that it will be to the Lord himself that I must give the ultimate account. Although there has been progress, I am still learning and still failing. It was not so long ago that I received an invitation to speak at what would be described by many people as a prestigious Christian event, but I was already booked at what seemed to me to be a much more ordinary event. After all my years of seeking to be a disciple of Jesus, there was still a battle – was I going to make my decision on the basis of having my name in lights today or would I make my decision in the light of 'that day'? In the end, I honoured the original booking.

Questions

1. If, like Martin Luther, we could say 'there are only two days in my diary, today and that day', how would that impact the daily decisions of our lives?
2. My experience of the church in poorer lands and areas where persecution is faced is that they think more of the Second Coming of Christ than we do in the freer and more wealthy countries in the West. Why do you think that might be?

Books

John Musgrave, *My Heart Will Choose To Say* (Milton Keynes: Authentic/Spring Harvest Publishing Division, 2005).

David Watson, *Fear No Evil* (London: Hodder & Stoughton, 1984).

Part Two

Whole life discipleship

Chapter Five

A disciple is a servant

'Jesus is Lord' is what I profess in the words of my creed but is my life lived out in his service?

If you knew you were going to die today, and you had the opportunity to speak with your closest friends, what would you talk about? Jesus had that opportunity (Jn. 13 – 16). What does he want to teach them at this critical time? How will he begin? He starts with the challenge to live a life of service rather than a life of self-serving. When Paul urges the church at Philippi to have the attitude of Jesus, it is his servant heart which he emphasises

> Your attitude should be the same as that of Christ Jesus:
> Who, being in very nature God,
> did not consider equality with God something to be
>   grasped,
> but made himself nothing,
> taking the very nature of a servant,
> being made in human likeness (Phil. 2:5–7).

I believe we have reached here the heart of the life of discipleship. Jesus brought glory to his Father through his

> Jesus brought glory to his Father through his self-giving love.

self-giving love. Now we have the opportunity to continue the glorifying of the Father through lives poured out for him and for those for whom Jesus died.

Washing the disciples' feet

Jesus and his disciples are having supper. These disciples have now been with Jesus for three years; listening to him, watching him. A surprising thing now takes place or, more accurately, fails to take place. Proper etiquette demands that guests, who would have tired, dusty feet from the journey, should have their feet washed before taking food. But there is a problem: this is not a pleasant task. Just come with me into any OM men's dorm and you will understand! This task is reserved for the servant in the house but there is no servant available. Who is going to take the lowly place? Who is sufficiently secure to serve? Who is so sure about his own position that he can be freed up to serve?

You can imagine the embarrassed tension as everyone waits for everyone else but nobody moves. Then, in what must have been a moment the disciples would never forget, Jesus rises, makes preparation, and washes their feet. Peter, it seems, is embarrassed. 'Lord, are you going to wash my feet?' (Jn. 13:6). Let's just take a step back for a moment. Those who are having their feet washed are very ordinary people, tax gatherers, fishermen. The foot washer is described as the One who 'had come from God and was returning to God' (Jn. 13:3). In a few days he will say, 'All authority in heaven and on earth has been given to me' (Mt. 28:18). The man who opened the eyes of the blind, the ears of the deaf and even gave life to the dead, is washing the feet of his own disciples. What the disciples were unwilling to do for each other, Jesus is doing for all of them.

He tells the disciples why he did this for them: 'I have set you an example that you should do as I have done for you' (Jn. 13:15). Jesus was saying to them, and he says to us, 'This is how I want you to live. I want you to be towel grabbers – constantly looking for opportunities to take the towel of service.' If we refuse to live this way, we are making quite a statement, placing ourselves above the Master. 'Now that I, your Lord and Teacher, have washed your feet, you also should wash one another's feet' (Jn. 13:14). Remember the dictionary definition of a disciple: 'One who takes another as his teacher and model.' Clearly to fail to live this life of service is to refuse the call to discipleship.

As Jesus washes his disciples' feet, he is doing more than setting an example. This was a symbolic act. Jesus is cleansing the dirty feet of his disciples with water but he will go from this supper to provide cleansing for dirty lives, by the giving of his life. That is why Jesus says to Peter; 'You do not realize now what I am doing, but later you will understand' (Jn. 13:7). This foot washing was symbolic of the greatest act of service this planet will ever witness.

Having the attitude of Christ

As we have seen when Paul wrote to the church in Philippi, he made it very clear that this is our supreme example. 'Your attitude should be the same as that of Christ Jesus' (Phil. 2:5). The Authorized Version translates that as 'Let this mind be in you which was also in

**Let this mind be in you
which was also in Christ
Jesus.**

Christ Jesus.' So how are we to think as Christ's disciples? If we are to think right, we must have at the forefront of our minds that Jesus, though 'being in very nature God, did not consider equality with God something to be grasped, but made himself nothing, taking the very nature of a servant.' With that servant heart, 'he humbled himself and became obedient to death – even death on a cross!' (Phil. 2:8).

This is vital teaching from Paul because it helps us to understand the mind of Christ as he approached the cross. What drove him forward? Paul tells us there was no thought of position or power in his mind. He was 'in very nature God' but he did not consider this equality with God 'something to be grasped.' He 'made himself nothing.'

> From heaven you came, helpless babe,
> Entered our world your glory veiled,
> Not to be served but to serve
> and give your life that we might live.
> This is our God, the Servant King,
> He calls us now to follow him
> To give our lives as a daily offering
> Of worship to the Servant King.
>
> *Copyright © Graham Kendrick 1983*
> *Thankyou Music tym@kingsway.co.uk*

Service was in the mind of Jesus as he approached the cross: the opportunity to serve his Father and humanity was at the forefront of his mind. How could Jesus live like this and how can we? 'Jesus knew that the Father

Writing about a baptism, missonary Jim Elliot wrote:

'My flesh often lacks the deep feeling that I should experience at such times and there was a certain dryness to the form this morning, but I cannot stay for feelings. So cold is my heart most of the time that I am almost always operating on the basis of pure commandments, forcing myself to do what I do not always feel, simply because I am a servant under orders.'

Elisabeth Elliot,
The Shadow of the Almighty
(Milton Keynes: Authentic Classics, 1997)

had put all things under his power, and that he had come from God and was returning to God' (Jn. 13:3). In other words, Jesus knew who he was. We might find doing the lowly tasks difficult because we are concerned what impact it might have on our image. 'What is it going to do for my credibility if I am seen cleaning the church toilets? That is hardly what you would expect to see someone aspiring to leadership in the church doing.' But Jesus would see things very differently.

I have a number of titles at present, because of what I am doing in Christian ministry. In the next few years I will lose these titles, as I do not believe those in leadership should hold on to their positions for too long. How will I feel when all the titles are gone? There is one title I will take into eternity. I am a child of God! I don't think that title can be improved on. Nothing surely gives greater dignity than that. When we realise who we are, we are freed to truly serve. There is no further need to make a name for ourselves or to worry about our image. We have a position that cannot be improved on and can never be removed from us.

Serving our enemies

In the strength of knowing who he was, Jesus came to Judas Iscariot. Jesus knew of his decision to betray him (Jn. 13:11). Will he pass him by? Surely we are not called to serve our betrayers? But no feet are missed. That is our calling; it is the call to discipleship; the call to follow the One who grabbed the towel and served even his betrayer. It is a comparatively easy thing to serve those who appreciate our service and may even serve us in return. But the scriptural standard is far higher.

A few years ago I endured what was unquestionably my most difficult year in Christian ministry. To use common language, a brother was 'out to get me.' I believe he was very sincere, but had completely misunderstood some of my actions. Nothing I could say or do would convince him that I was for him. He was convinced I was against him and at all costs I had to go. If I was to be true to the biblical standard, I had to go out of my way to serve him. Was it possible? I cannot say I succeeded on all occasions, but Jesus does not call us to do something that is impossible. Without faith, without the gifts of the Holy Spirit, such living is totally impossible, but those gifts are ours and so that is our calling.

Questions

1. Do you have the equivalent of a Judas in your life and is God calling you to wash their feet?
2. Look at the diagrams over the page and fill in where you serve already. Then spend some time praying and ask God how he would like to see the diagrams change.

Books

Fran Beckett, *Rebuild* (Leicester: Crossway books, 2001).

Example: your commitments might look like this:

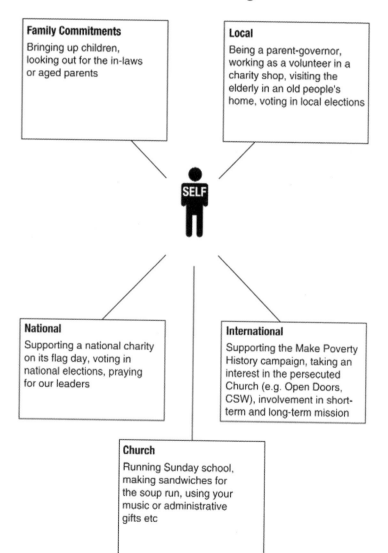

Family Commitments
Bringing up children, looking out for the in-laws or aged parents

Local
Being a parent-governor, working as a volunteer in a charity shop, visiting the elderly in an old people's home, voting in local elections

National
Supporting a national charity on its flag day, voting in national elections, praying for our leaders

International
Supporting the Make Poverty History campaign, taking an interest in the persecuted Church (e.g. Open Doors, CSW), involvement in short-term and long-term mission

Church
Running Sunday school, making sandwiches for the soup run, using your music or administrative gifts etc

Where are you serving? Where else is God calling you to serve?

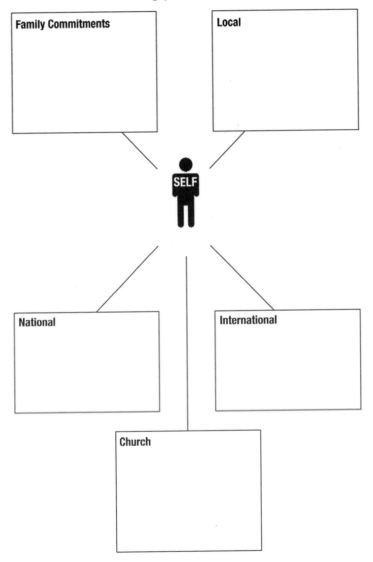

Family Commitments

Local

SELF

National

International

Church

Chapter Six

A disciple is a steward

It was in my late teens that I was first challenged by surely one of the most remarkable statements Jesus ever made; 'any of you who does not give up everything he has cannot be my disciple' (Lk. 14:33). At first, I thought it was just a bit too much. So I tried a few other translations to see if they lessened the impact. I even tried the Greek but nothing helped. It seems that this really is what Jesus said. To follow him, to be his disciple, everything must go. Initially, I thought Jesus was speaking just about people's possessions, and I am sure that is part of what was in his mind, but a lot more than our possessions must go if we are going to truly follow Jesus.

> Any of you who does not give up everything he has cannot be my disciple.

Profit and loss

I mentioned briefly in Chapter One that when Paul began to appreciate who Jesus really was, it changed the whole perspective of his life. He wrote 'whatever was to my profit I now consider loss for the sake of Christ' (Phil. 3:7). He actually wrote that he had lost all things for Christ and he considered the things that he had lost (which had previously been the things he lived for) were now rubbish (Phil. 3:8).

It is almost as though Paul is writing as an accountant in this passage. He had been accumulating what he considered was considerable profit for many years. His birth and his circumcision on the eighth day of his life had brought to him full possession of the covenant blessings of the people of God. He was 'of the tribe of Benjamin' (Phil. 3:5), the tribe which gave the first king of Israel and alone remained loyal to David and his successors. When he writes of being a 'Hebrew born of Hebrews' (v5), he may have been referring to the heritage he had received from his zealously religious parents. But it was not just inherited profit: he had increased his profit by his own actions. He had become a Pharisee, totally committed to keeping God's law in the smallest detail. He was so convinced and committed that he would oppose anyone who challenged what had become his absolute conviction. So when the church began to grow, he was found 'persecuting the church' (v6). Finally summarizing all this, he writes 'as for legalistic righteousness, faultless' (v6). His parents had done everything for him required by the law and he had continued by diligent observance of that law. He was genuinely convinced that if you had been able to look at the balance sheet of his life at that moment it was overwhelmingly in profit.

Then he met the man he had been convinced was dead. There was an almighty crash in his world of profit and loss. Everything in the profit column was suddenly

He had gained Christ.

transferred to the loss column. But, amazingly, Paul found himself far richer than he had ever been or ever imagined that he could have been. He had gained Christ (v8) and found profit in him that could never be added to.

When Jesus teaches this crowd that they must give up everything they have to follow him, he is developing what he has said about the necessity of cross bearing and of dying to self. Everything must go; all that we previously relied upon, the things that we took pride in. We must now see such things as rubbish. Paul writes to the Galatians 'May I never boast except in the cross of our Lord Jesus Christ, through which the world has been crucified to me, and I to the world' (Gal. 6:14).

Can I afford this?

Unless we realise what it takes to be a true follower of Jesus, we are likely to be very soon embarrassed or easily defeated. Jesus uses two brief parables (Lk. 14:28–32) to make these two points before issuing the challenge to give up everything. If you are going to build a tower, you don't just buy a few bricks and start building. If you do, you are probably going to finish up with an unfinished building and a lot of people very amused as they walk by. It makes sense to do some planning to realise the time and effort and resources it's going to take before you begin. If you watch these TV property programmes where people find an old house and, with great enthusiasm, begin to renovate it, you will know how often they

Are our hearts set on the new kind of life that Jesus offers, or on the quick comforts of the consumer lifestyle? Like an inner compass, our innermost longings set direction for our lives. Do we find our passions and energies, our dreams and desires, drawn towards the mercy and justice of God, or towards our own comfort? Whichever is the case, whichever direction our hearts are set towards, the journey of our life will be affected. And the heart, more often than not, follows the eyes.

Gerard Kelly, Humanifesto
(Milton Keynes: Spring Harvest Publishing Division/Authentic Media, 2001)

The cost of following Jesus must never be minimized.

fail to plan properly. They invariably find it takes more time and money than they thought it would. The cost of following Jesus must never be minimized. I think if some preachers were selling goods they would be guilty of breaking the Trades Descriptions Act.

We need to ask – 'Can I afford to follow Jesus?' But there is a more important question: 'Can I afford not to follow Jesus?' If a king is planning war, his opponent has to make plans to defend himself and his people, otherwise he is allowing disaster even when he has the opportunity to avert it. The consequences of not following Jesus are far too serious. While that is certainly the case, we still cannot follow without planning. If the king being attacked knows his opponent is bringing twenty thousand troops to the battle and he just recruits ten thousand, his defeat may well be quick.

Giving up everything

Following Jesus takes all the resources we've got. He is worthy of everything we have to give. Our enemy is so strong and subtle that less than everything committed to the battle will inevitably lead to early defeat. So Jesus says to the crowd following him, many of whom I think were curious spectators rather than serious followers, 'In the same way, any of you who does not give up everything he has cannot be my disciple' (Lk. 14:33). I wonder how many of the crowd walked away at that point.

And yet I am still a house owner and I drive a very comfortable car, and I haven't walked away from Jesus!

We cannot but serve our treasures. We labour all day for them and think about them all night. They fill our dreams. But it is not uncommon for people to think that they can treasure this world and an invisible kingdom as well, that they can serve both. Perhaps we can make this work for a while. But there will come a time when one must be subordinate to the other. We simply cannot have two ultimate goals or points of reference for our actions. That is how life is, and no one escapes. You cannot be the servant of both God and things 'on earth' because their requirements conflict. Unless you have already put God first, for example, what you will have to do to be financially secure, impress other people, or fulfil your desires will inevitably lead you against God's wishes. That is why the first of the Ten Commandments, 'You shall have no gods who take priority over me,' is the first of the Ten Commandments.

Dallas Willard, The Divine Conspiracy
(London: HarperCollins, 1998)

I said I don't think Jesus was only referring to possessions but that was certainly included. So am I living in disobedience? I don't think so and I certainly hope I'm not. But it is a daily challenge to live in obedience in this area in our consumer age. My name is on the registration document of the car I drive and I recently paid off my mortgage, yet Jesus is Lord!

My life is his; he is my rightful Owner, by creation and redemption, and everything I have is his. I am called to steward or to manage these things for his glory. This does not mean I can never use the things that God gives me for my own enjoyment. Paul is clear that it is God 'who richly provides us with everything for our enjoyment' (1 Tim. 6:17). It also does not mean that everything I have belongs to everyone else. One of the lessons we can learn from the sad demise of Ananias and Sapphira is that they had every right to own the piece of land they possessed, and when they sold it and gave a gift to the apostles, there was no compulsion for them to give everything. They had every right to hold back whatever they thought was appropriate.

Our ownership and our use of what God entrusts to us must recognise his Lordship over everything we are and have. It must recognise that we no longer live for ourselves: death has taken place and we live now for him. That house I now possess I have every right to enjoy, but I must ask – 'How does God want me to use it?' Should the spare room be available for someone who has hit a particularly hard time? It has quite a large front room, so is this the place where the church's small group needs be located? What God wants you to do with your house

Are we bringing everything we have to him?

It would be simpler if Christians were called to vows of poverty. If we knew that it was God's will that none of us own cars; that all of us were allowed precisely two sets of underwear, one set of outerwear and $50 a month rent, one pair of slippers and one pair of shoes, we would all know where we stood. But Jesus does not make it that easy. His teaching about giving away a second suit is not an attempt to set maximum living standards.

John White, The Cost of Commitment *(Leicester: IVP, 1976)* will probably be very different from what he wants me to do with mine. But the question is: are we bringing everything we have to him with this attitude of stewardship; this understanding that we now live, and use everything we have, with the desire for his glory? Everything must be submitted to his Lordship. 'Jesus is Lord' was the simple but utterly radical first Christian creed.

Questions

1. 'Any of you who does not give up everything he has cannot be my disciple.' Is there anything that comes to your mind as you meditate on that statement that you know you must give up?
2. What is God asking you to do with what you own?

   - List all your possessions – house, car, tools, washing machine … (leave out obvious things that cannot be lent)
   - Then pray – how can I use all this for others?
   - For instance – Can I use my home for hospitality? For foreign students? For the vulnerable? For fostering?
   - Can I lend my car? Can I give people lifts? Can I help with their shopping?
   - Can I lend my tools? Can I share my books? Can I take some stuff I don't need to a charity shop?

Books

Richard Foster, *Money, Sex and Power* (London: Hodder & Stoughton, 1999).

Neil Hood, *God's Wealth – Whose Money is it Anyway?* (Milton Keynes: Authentic, 2004).

Peter Maiden, *Take My Plastic* (Carlisle: Authentic, 1997).

Rob Parsons, *The Money Secret* (London: Hodder & Stoughton, 2005).

John White, *The Golden Cow* (STL, 1980).

John Rowell, *To Give or Not to Give: Generosity and the Dependency Myth* (Milton Keynes: Authentic, 2007).

Chapter Seven

Sex

In a *Newsweek* cover story entitled 'What Teens Believe,' Rob Rienow, a youth minister at Wheaton Bible Church, Wheaton, Illinois, stated, 'Their answers were as individual as the kids themselves. One thought God was like their grandfather, "He's there but I never see him." Another took a harder view, describing 'an evil being who wants to punish me all the time.' Two more opinions followed. Finally, the last teen weighed in: 'I think you're all right, because that's what you really believe.' In other words, as Rienow relates it, God is whatever works for you. On this, all of the youth agreed.

Josh McDowell introduces us to Amber 'a typical sixteen-year old Christian from a solid youth group.' He asks her 'Is it wrong to engage in premarital sex?' 'Well, I believe it's wrong for me,' she responds. McDowell probes further: 'But do you believe the Bible teaches that premarital sex is wrong for everyone?'

'Amber's eyes shift back and forth as she weighs her answer. "Well," she begins slowly, "I know it's wrong for me, and I have chosen not to have sex until I'm married. But I don't think I can judge other people on what they do."'[8]

The Maker's instructions

'Jesus is Lord' means that there are absolutes that govern the behaviour of all God's people at all times. When it comes to our sexual behaviour, Paul does not give his opinion but gives 'instructions by the authority of the Lord Jesus' (1 Thess. 4:2). The word translated 'instructions' is a strong word, which in Paul's day would have been used for a military command or a court order. However counter cultural it may be when it comes to our sexual behaviour, if we are to be disciples of Jesus, it is not a question of 'Doing what seems right at the time' or 'Doing what seems natural' but of obedience to the clear and definite instructions which the Lord Jesus has given us.

What are those instructions? We will discover them as we look at the verses which follow but first it is vital to recognise the positive context in which they are given. 'It is God's will that you should be sanctified' (1 Thess. 4:3). A friend of mine was having difficulty in her marriage, particularly in the sexual area. She went to see a counsellor

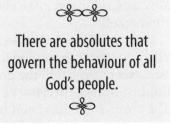

There are absolutes that govern the behaviour of all God's people.

who was not a professing Christian. As she explained the issues, it wasn't long before the counsellor was asking 'Excuse me, but are you a born again Christian?' When she made it clear she was, the counsellor continued 'I am not surprised. I find so many who come to me are, and they get totally hung up in this area of sex.' Somehow we have contrived to make this beautiful gift of our generous Father an issue that we are embarrassed to talk about and it leaves us feeling slightly dirty. The

Bible has a great deal to say about our sexual behaviour but how often do you hear the subject clearly and practically taught in our churches? The first time I mentioned masturbation in my own church, I think people thought the walls would fall down, but it is one of the most common and intense sexual issues that we have to deal with.

Joyce Huggett was writing a book on relationships on the island of Cyprus. She describes how one day she was in the bath when there was an earthquake. As she ran out of the bathroom, she said the thought came to her mind; 'Jesus has come – he's returned!' She continues 'The initial excitement evaporated as I looked down on my naked body. Oh, no! He can't choose this minute. I'm naked, I'm naked and I'm still dripping wet.' She says the lesson she learned was that though she had been telling audiences for years what the Bible says about sex, telling thousands to accept their bodies and their sexuality as God-given gifts, she had not reached that maturity herself.

Do you believe that Jesus was sexually tempted? If you don't, you are saying that he had every human emotion except probably the greatest emotion of all. He was hungry, thirsty, tired but never touched by sexual desire! The truth is he 'has been tempted in every way, just as we are – yet was without sin' (Heb. 4:15).

God's will for us is our sanctification, that we should live holy lives. Holy lives please God. What comes to your mind when you think of living a holy life? Is it stained glass windows, and monasteries? Possibly your view is not that extreme, but I wonder if you think of a truly exciting fulfilling life? Do you

> **Holy lives please God.**

admire the life of Jesus? Do you believe that to live as he lived would be to truly live? It certainly seems the people who were around Jesus at the time found his life to be extremely attractive. I am sure that he was the most interesting, engaging, fascinating, stimulating human being who has ever lived. Jesus lived a holy life and made it clear that that is his desire for his followers. He also said 'I have come that they (his followers) may have life and have it to the full' (Jn. 10:10). This was in contrast to 'the thief' who 'comes only to steal and kill and destroy.' Satan's great lie is that his way opens the door to true satisfaction and that it is God who is the killjoy. The reality is that Satan is the thief and the killer and God is the generous Giver who wants his followers to live life to the full.

Handle with care

I am afraid it is an all too common experience to sit in my office with a weeping Christian who has believed that lie and is paying the consequences. Often the lie has been fed to them in this area of sex; an area where the thief particularly likes to steal from us. God, through the gift of sex, has given such potential for pleasure and satisfaction. The thief hates the very thought of the people of God having such enjoyment, and of God having

God, through the gift of sex, has given such potential for pleasure.

such joy in their enjoyment, so he will steal that joy, kill that pleasure and turn this beautiful gift into a total nightmare.

. . . the key elements of marriage (leaving, uniting, becoming one flesh) do not require the emotional state that the modern media insist is the only basis for marriage. In fact in an arranged marriage 'being in love' was either the icing on the cake or something that came later. The emphasis in marriage lay elsewhere. This may seem strange and even heartless to us, but it had its merits. The point is this: 'feeling in love' with someone is in fact what it says – a feeling. And a feeling, even a strong one, on its own may fade. To hold a marriage together over many years, a better glue than emotions is needed. God knows this. That's why he wants marriage to be broadly based and bound by promises. Ironically, within the secure framework of marriage where other things are doing the cementing, the emotion of love may thrive and persist.

J.John, Ten – Living the Ten Commandments in the 21st Century *(Eastbourne: Kingsway, 2000)*

The strategy of the thief is to suggest that what God has said is the way to sexual fulfilment is just not the way. 'Why wait until marriage? It can't possibly do any harm, especially if we are already engaged. That's the proof of our commitment and what possible difference can one further piece of paper make?'

'I haven't gone looking for this, the emotion is just overwhelming. I can't help myself.' Those are the words of a married man who had made the decision to be unfaithful to his partner. We talk ourselves into the move that steals and kills. It steals from the person we are choosing to be with. It steals from our partner and often people will say later, 'Something died within me that day.'

G.K. Chesterton wrote; 'All healthy men (and I would add women) ancient and modern, Eastern and Western, know that there is a certain fury in sex that we cannot afford to inflame, and that a certain mystery and awe must ever surround it if we are to remain sane.' That is so true. This wonderful gift from God has a certain

Without appropriate discipline, this gift will burn and destroy.

fury and, without appropriate discipline, this gift will burn and destroy.

So after setting the positive context, Paul immediately moves to the need for discipline, not because sex is bad, but because it is so good and powerful that the potential for destruction is just as great as the potential for satisfaction. Sitting behind the wheel of a Ferrari, there are two potential outcomes for me – to have a great experience or to destroy myself and possibly many others in a moment. And one could lead to the other.

So what discipline is required to ensure that the gift of sex is satisfying rather than destructive? Paul asks the Thessalonians to do two things: 'Avoid sexual immorality and learn to control your body.' The word translated 'sexual immorality' means every kind of illicit sexual intercourse. For the Christian who wants to obey God, that can only mean one thing. The only sexual intercourse that God planned for us and which therefore will be truly satisfying is with our marriage partner. There are no exceptions to that, no special cases.

Some might of course say this is impossible in the 21st century. It sets the bar too high. It is so counter-cultural to live like this. In the UK today less than 1% of men and women have their first experience of sex with someone they are married or engaged to.[9] Isn't this such an outdated idea that it can no longer be valid?

We need to appreciate two things. God did not put any time limit on these commands. The Scriptures are valid for all people in all cultures at all times. The people whom Paul was writing to in Thessalonica were living in a culture just as promiscuous as ours. 'The cities of Greece, Asia Minor and Egypt had become centres of the wildest corruption. There has probably never been a period when vice was more extravagant or uncontrolled than it was under the Caesars.'[10] Prior to their conversion, immorality had probably played a part in the religious practices of many of these Thessalonian believers. If we think that to live like this in our culture is a huge challenge, it was no less of a challenge for them.

> The Scriptures are valid for all people in all cultures at all times.

So how can we live totally avoiding sexual immorality? We must 'learn to control our bodies.' In the context this can only mean our bodily or sexual desires. That is the challenge. We must learn to control one of the most powerful passions most of us will ever experience. After giving this instruction, Paul writes; 'He who rejects this instruction does not reject man but God, who gives you his Holy Spirit' (1 Thess. 4:8).

The eye and the mind

I am so grateful Paul mentions the Holy Spirit, because without his powerful enabling I cannot live in this way. A power greater than the powerful sexual drive is required and, thank God, that power is there, available to us, the power of God, the Holy Spirit. We are called to cooperate with the Holy Spirit if we are to live in purity. It is not just a question of turning on the power when we get into difficulty. We must obey the Holy Spirit and the word that the Holy Spirit inspired. Discipline must begin with the eye and the mind. There is no sexual failure that did not begin with an undisciplined eye and continue with an undisciplined mind. Today that indiscipline often finds expression in spending time on internet pornography sites. I was recently told that 12% of all sites are now of this nature and a quarter of all internet engine searches are to locate one of those sites. In some churches, surveys have shown that one in two people are spending time on these sites. It seems this is a problem of epidemic proportion. If we are serious about discipline in this area, we will build into our

Discipline must begin with the eye and the mind.

lives and our hardware safeguards and accountability arrangements.

We see a clear example of this in the story of King David and Bathsheba. Some people condemn King

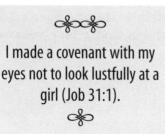

I made a covenant with my eyes not to look lustfully at a girl (Job 31:1).

David for sending out his troops under the leadership of Joab and staying home himself. But he had been leading his troops in battle for years and everyone, even the king, needs a break. Satan, however, is different; he doesn't seem to need a break and certainly never seems to take one.

David can't sleep. Is this the great leader, concerned for his men? He takes a walk on the palace roof and there he sees a beautiful woman, Bathsheba, bathing. Should we be critical of Bathsheba for the place she chooses? There is David's first opportunity; he can immediately walk back inside his palace. But I don't think he did. He stayed and he looked. It went beyond 'What a beautiful woman.' That powerful sexual drive was kicking in. David finally goes back inside the palace, but now his thoughts are raging. 'I'll send someone to find out who she is.' This is his second grave error. He has an opportunity to walk away, but the 'fury' is now burning and unless he takes action soon, it's going to hurt him and others.

The servant returns; 'Isn't this Bathsheba, the daughter of Eliam and the wife of Uriah the Hittite?' She's a married woman, so will he walk away now? But no. The way of escape was there on more than one occasion but he doesn't take it. Instead he takes the route that will

It is a high standard and we have all failed. There may well be things we have done of which we are deeply ashamed. If so, let us remember the good news of the gospel. Jesus did not just die for certain sins. If we have trusted in him, we have been forgiven for all that we have done wrong and are perfect in God's sight. Paul wrote these stern words to the Corinthians: 'Neither the sexually immoral nor idolaters nor adulterers nor male prostitutes nor homosexual offenders . . . will inherit the kingdom of God.' But then he added, 'And that is what some of you were. But you were washed, you were sanctified, you were justified in the name of the Lord Jesus Christ and by the Spirit of our God' (1 Cor. 6:9–11).

Vaughan Roberts, Distinctives *(Milton Keynes: Authentic, 2003), p. 67*

> ❧❧
>
> It is impossible for you to maintain a pure mind if you are a television watching couch potato. In one week you will watch more murders, adulteries and perversions than our grandfathers read about in their entire lives.
>
> *Kent Hughes*
>
> ❧

lead to devastation for Bathsheba, her husband Uriah and to permanent scarring for David himself.

The Psalms help us to understand some of the emotions of this incident. It was only after the baby was born from this adulterous act that David repented, when confronted by Nathan. For at least nine months he was living with unconfessed sin. 'When I kept silent, my bones wasted away through my groaning all day long. For day and night your hand was heavy upon me; my strength was sapped as in the heat of summer' (Ps. 32:3–4). Some interpreters suggest that David wrote those words during that nine month period. After he finally confesses his sin, he cries out to God; 'Restore to me the joy of your salvation' (Ps. 51:12). The thief has been at work, robbing David of his strength and his joy.

David crossed a line when he sent for Bathsheba. Back in 1 Thessalonians 4, Paul writes; 'In this matter no-one should wrong his brother or take advantage of him' (v6). John Stott writes; 'The first verb has the force

> ❧❧
>
> We have all been there.
>
> ❧

of crossing a boundary – here of crossing a forbidden boundary, and hence trespassing (sexually) on territory which is not your own, while the second verb is the desire to possess more than one should in any area of life.'[11] If someone tells you they have never been drawn to that line, check their pulse! We have all been there, but God is there with us and we do not need to cross that line. The desire is not uncontrollable; that is a devilish suggestion. By the power of the Holy Spirit, we can live in purity, even in 21st century culture. We can look away; we can walk away in the power of the Holy Spirit.

There is a way back

Some of you are feeling this is all irrelevant, because you have already failed, and the thief loves to say what you've lost, you've lost forever. He's lying again: not surprisingly, as he is 'the father of lies.' David's joy and strength were restored after his repentance. There was ongoing damage in his life, but he knew the power of the Holy Spirit in his life again, and he knew what it was to be useful once more in the service of his God. Sexual sin can have grave consequences for others and ourselves but don't let anyone suggest to you that it is the unforgivable sin.

Some after sexual sin know they are forgiven, they know the doctrine and the theory of forgiveness, but they find it very difficult to accept the reality emotionally. God may have forgiven them, but can they forgive themselves? I spoke to a young man who had failed in this area and he said; 'I knew God loved me but I didn't think he liked me.' He certainly didn't like himself. Gradually, however, he saw that he had been imposing an identity on himself: 'I am a moral failure.' Through counselling he began to realise that: that what he had *done* was not who he *was*. What he had done had been brought to the cross and the blood of Christ had atoned

Leadership magazine commissioned a poll of a thousand pastors. The pastors indicated that twelve per cent of them had committed adultery while in the ministry, that is one out of eight pastors, and twenty-three per cent had done something they considered sexually inappropriate.[12]

Christianity Today magazine surveyed a thousand of its subscribers who were not pastors, and twenty-three per cent said they had had extramarital intercourse, with forty-five per cent indicating they had done something they themselves deemed sexually inappropriate. That is one in four Christian men are unfaithful and almost fifty per cent have behaved in a way they themselves consider inappropriate.[13]

for it, along with all his other sins. He was and he is a son of God. He knew moral failure, but God no longer sees that failure. His sins had been 'hurled into the depths of the sea.' He is a child of God: that is his identity and God loves and likes his children.

Questions

1. 'There is a certain fury in sex.' Is there any aspect of your life where you are currently playing with fire?
2. 'There is no sexual failure that did not begin with an undisciplined eye and continue with an undisciplined mind.' Think about that statement and then ask yourself whether there are any actions you need to take in the light of it?

Books

Elisabeth Elliott, *Passion and Purity* (Carlisle: Authentic, 1994).

Richard Foster, *Money, Sex and Power* (London: Hodder & Stoughton, 1999).

Dr Tony and Anne Hobbs, *Marriage Masterclass* (Milton Keynes: Authentic 2002).

Nigel Pollock, *Relationships Revolution* (Leicester: IVP, 1998).

Vaughan Roberts, *Battles Christians Face* (Milton Keynes: Authentic, 2007).

John White, *Eros Defiled* (Leicester: IVP, 1977).

Chapter Eight

Money

Is consumerism the religion of the twenty-first century? The shopping centre is now the place of worship for many on a Sunday morning. Tony Walter has written a book, whose title seems to sum up the present situation: *Need: The New Religion.*[14]

Andrew Walker writes; 'Begun in the 1940s by Henry Ford, consumerism became the dominant cultural force of the last half of the twentieth century. After the second world war, rising standards of living, full employment, technological advance and innovative marketing spearheaded the American revolution, that has led to its cultural dominance and imitation since.' It is vital if we are to understand this culture that we realise the ability and capacity to supply goods far outstrips the demand for those goods. The only way to keep the 'show on the road' is to sell us what we do not really need and to ensure that many of the things sold to us wear out quickly.

> If you 'have', you are deemed a success.

We are therefore bombarded constantly with the

'Must have' message. If you 'have', you are deemed a success: if you don't, well, how can you live without it? Our 'flexible friends' stand by so that we can 'have' even when we 'don't have.'

This is creating an increasingly divided world of the 'haves' and the 'have nots.' For many people, tragically their self worth is to some degree dependent on their ability to purchase. So people will work the kind of hours that damage other areas of their lives, or run up debts that will ultimately become a huge burden, in order to be up with the crowd. The prophets of our consumer age drone on, promising that all you need for ultimate satisfaction is the latest gizmo but it is like drinking sea water: the more we fall for the lie, the more thirsty we become.

The apostle Paul wrote one sentence that sends the leaders of this consumer age scurrying to emergency committee meetings: 'I have learned in whatever state I am to be content.' If that idea becomes popular, it will sound the death knell to consumerism!

How are we to follow Jesus in this consumer age? I have a hero, who's neither a missionary nor a vicar! He

> I have learned in whatever state I am to be content.

is a businessman, and a successful one – yes, it is possible to be successful in business and a Christian. I have known this man for many years and during those years, his income has increased considerably. His business has gone from strength to strength, but remarkably his lifestyle hardly seems to have altered. He lives in the same home as he did when his business was quite small. It is a very pleasant home and his lifestyle certainly includes a few things that some would deem to be luxuries. But the point

The good life of advertisements is eating a chocolate bar on a sun-kissed beach in paradise. It's being two stone lighter, or looking twenty years younger. It's what you wear, or what you have. It's the holiday of a lifetime, the feel of an expensive luxury car, or a sip of an exclusive brandy. It's owning a dream cottage in the country. This 'good life' is a hotchpotch of hedonism (just do it), escapism (the holiday location always looks better in the brochure), and materialism (shop till you drop).

More money is currently spent on advertising than on education, so in terms of influence advertising executives are our primary educators. They are successful, and therefore highly paid, teachers. We trust their message – and go out and buy their stuff. Millions of us are working harder, longer hours as we chase the good life.

Dallas Willard

that has fascinated me is that his lifestyle decisions have not been determined by his income. I have so rarely witnessed anyone living like this. The message of this consumer age is; 'If you have it, you have every right to spend it, and you need to spend it to truly live.' This man has it, but he doesn't spend it, he gives it. He gives it to a variety of Christian ministries and a number of those ministries would struggle to continue without his generosity. He is my hero because he has been looking at life over all these years through the eyes of Christ and I think the business world is probably one of the most difficult to do that in.

I have had the privilege over the years of meeting and spending time with some rich Christians. I have lived in the homes of a number. Some of them have been wonderful examples of this stewardship principle. They have not given the impression; 'Look how well I've done. This is all mine through my ability and hard work.' They have had an attitude of gratitude to God, for the abilities they have been given, the strength to use those abilities and a concern to use what they have been given for the glory of God. Paul has some encouraging words for such people. If the rich resist arrogance, put their hope in God rather than their always uncertain wealth, and are rich in good deeds, generous and willing to share, then 'they will lay up treasure for themselves as a firm foundation for the coming age, so that they may take hold of the life that is truly life' (1 Tim. 6:19).

God the generous Giver

So let us consider some vital principles for Christian disciples in this area. The most well known verse in the Bible (Jn. 3:16) is probably the most vital here; 'God so loved the world that he gave his only Son.' Our God is a

Our God is a Giver, not a hoarder.

Giver, not a hoarder. He gives generously, even extravagantly. I remember a particular period when our children were quite young and money was in short supply. When they came asking for things, I tried to respond but I was a real 'bean counter' and I gave them the bare minimum. That is not the way God gives. 'And the LORD God made all kinds of trees grow out of the ground – trees that were pleasing to the eye and good for food' (Gen. 2:9). The land he gave to his people Israel was a land 'flowing with milk and honey' (Num. 14:8). The life that Jesus came to this earth to obtain for us is an abundant life – a life to be lived to the full (Jn. 10:10). The salvation we have in Jesus is not by the skin of our teeth since 'he is able to save completely those who come to God through him' (Heb. 7:25). Paul reckoned it was impossible to grasp all the extravagance that God has prepared for his people. 'No eye has seen, no ear has heard, no mind has conceived what God has prepared for those who love him' (1 Cor. 2:9).

I do want to overemphasise this point, because I believe it is so vital to living right in this consumer age. 'A disciple is some one who takes someone else as his model and example:' if we are to live lives of discipleship in this consumer age, then we must understand the generosity of our God and be imitators of him.

In such an age, it may appear heroic to be givers rather than spenders. But it is not at all. It is one of the basic principles of following Jesus that, if we want to save our lives then we must lose them. It is one of the principles of his upside-down kingdom. This is the kingdom where the weak are strong, the poor are rich and the dead truly live. It is also the kingdom where the receivers are the givers.

Give all you can

In his book *Joy in Ministry*, Michael Duduit tells a story of J.C. Stribling and the 1929 stock market crash in America. Prior to the depression Stribling was a wealthy Texas rancher. He owned a great deal of land, thousands of head of cattle and a fortune in stocks and bonds. During this time he gave $150,000 to build a girls' dormitory on the campus of Mary Harding-Baylor College, a Baptist college in Texas.

Then came the depression. Stribling lost his entire fortune. He was reduced to virtual poverty. One day in 1933 a man came to the side of Stribling's old run-down Ford and spoke to Stribling and his wife. Pastor Brandon explained that he had just returned from driving a group of girls to enrol in the college. He had spent a night there and now wanted to thank Mr Stribling for his gift of the college. Stribling was silent for a few moments as his eyes filled with tears. Then he spoke, 'That was all we saved out of a mighty fortune. It was

Preacher, tell the people to give all they can to the Kingdom of God while they have it.

what we gave away that we were able to keep forever.'[15] Then he added this challenge, 'Preacher, tell people to give all they can to the Kingdom of God while they have it. I wish I had given more.'

The principle of the consumer age is: if you have it, spend it. The discipleship principle is, if you have it, it is a gift to you from God, a gift to enjoy, but the only way you will truly enjoy the gift is to give it back. If he is the Lord of my life, then everything I have is his. Before I understood this principle, there was only one question when it came to issues of purchase. Did I have enough to buy the item I wanted? Now there are two questions. 'Do I have enough?' and 'Lord, all that I am and have is yours: do you want me to have this item for my enjoyment, for "he gives us all things richly to enjoy?" Do you want me to have it so that I might use it to further your interests in this world? I am here to use what you give me for your glory.'

Our attitude to material things, particularly in this consumer age, is very indicative of where our priorities lie in our discipleship. Someone has said we worship God just as much with our chequebook as we do with our hymnbook. I am sure that is true and it must also be true that the worship expressed through our chequebook is a little more quantifiable than that of our hymnbook! Paul writes to the church in Corinth; 'I want to test the sincerity of your love by comparing it with the earnestness of others' (2 Cor. 8:8). He is looking for donations from the Corinthian church for a collection he is making for Christians in Jerusalem who have been hit by famine. He has already received donations from the very poor churches of Macedonia and what they gave proved their love. 'Now', he writes to the Corinthians, 'How much do you love? One way I will see the answer to that is how much you give.'

> We worship God just as much with our chequebook as we do with our hymnbook.

That of course would not just be the amount, but the amount in comparison to what they had and also the manner in which they gave. Did they give grudgingly? Did they give out of a sense of duty? Was their giving a joyous expression of their love for God and

If you give God everything you have, he will provide everything you need.

Anon

for their brothers and sisters in Jerusalem? It has been said that the important issue is not how much we give but how much we keep. Are we going to be a follower of Jesus at this very practical point? Jesus is the example that Paul holds out before the Corinthians. 'For you know the grace of our Lord Jesus Christ, that though he was rich, yet for your sakes he became poor, so that you through his poverty might become rich' (2 Cor. 8:9).

Giving principles

I write as a western Christian and in global terms I am very rich. As far as my income is concerned, I am in the top 10% in the world. This leaves me with huge responsibilities. Paul is looking for donations from Corinth because of the needs in famine-hit Jerusalem. The principle is; 'At the present time your plenty will supply what they need, so that in turn their plenty will supply what you need. Then there will be equality' (2 Cor. 8:14). One of the

The important issue is not how much we give but how much we keep.

huge challenges of daily life is to know how I should live in the light of this teaching. I have sought to do what my business friend has done, ensuring that my lifestyle decisions are not influenced by my income (which has been very inconsistent over the years) but by conviction and principles. There have been certain gizmos which I have decided I can definitely live quite happily without, only to find concerned Christian friends coming to my door with them as gifts because they didn't want me to suffer because I was in paid Christian work! Gradually, as with many other areas of my discipleship, I am growing to a position with which I am more settled. My position is based on principles, so let me share the principles with you because 'principles are timeless', while practice may change according to our situation.

So, to summarise: God is a giving God and I want to be like him. I don't want to be stingy; I want to be generous, open handed. Secondly, it is good to give. Dr Luke tells us that Jesus said; 'It is more blessed to give than to receive.' It is a liberating truth that every time a gift is given, both the receiver and the giver are blessed. Working as I have done for most of my life for 'faith missions' who have relied upon the generosity of donors, I know the blessing of receiving but Scripture is clear that the giver will enjoy even greater blessing. Thirdly, a broken world and a hurting body needs generous givers. In the Body of Christ we are to 'bear one another's burdens' (Gal. 6:2). I know that generous giving can do a lot of burden bearing in the Body of Christ. Then, finally, the broken world is clear to all; the question is not is there a need for giving

God is giving God and I want to be like him.

but where best can my giving be focused to make the maximum impact?

How much should you give if you are to be a true disciple of Jesus? As we have seen, the answer is 'Everything!' He is Lord, we are his, and we submit everything we have to his

We make a living by what we get. We make a life by what we give.
Duane Hulse

Lordship. That is a vital principle, but what about detailed practice? When the wage is paid into your bank, how much do you give away and how much do you keep?

No-one can answer that question for you. It is a personal issue you must work through in your relationship with your Lord. But as you work it through, remember these principles. Firstly, don't rob God. All of it is his, so don't hold anything back. Secondly, your giving will be in proportion to your income. Jesus spoke more about money than he did about sexual immorality or about hell. And it is an uncomfortable truth that if we are living in the same way as those around us who earn similar salaries, and our giving makes no difference to this, then we may well not be giving enough. Giving is meant to be sacrificial; it is meant to make an impact on our lifestyles.

Questions

1. In this chapter, we have considered the using of our money as disciples of Jesus. But what about how we earn that money? Are there jobs and even industries that are barred to the Christian?
2. 'It was what we were able to give away that we were able to keep forever.' Think about that statement. Do you have a 'giving plan'? If not, should you decide to work one out or should you revise the one you have?

Further study – Find a concordance and look up every Bible reference to money (or do it on Bible Gateway, on a keyword search).

Books

Richard Foster, *Money, Sex and Power* (London: Hodder & Stoughton, 1999).

Neil Hood, *God's Wealth – Whose Money is it Anyway?* (Milton Keynes: Authentic, 2004).

Peter Maiden, *Take My Plastic* (Carlisle: Authentic, 1997).

Rob Parsons, *The Money Secret* (London: Hodder & Stoughton, 2005).

Ronald Sider, *Rich Christians in an Age of Hunger*. There are various editions of this, either new and revised, or secondhand from Amazon.

John White, *The Golden Cow* (STL, 1980).

Chapter Nine

Time

In Ephesians 5:15 Paul writes; 'Be very careful then, how you live – not as unwise but as wise.' If we are doing so, the first evidence that will be seen, according to Paul, is in our use of time: 'making the most of every opportunity, because the days are evil' (v16). The Authorized Version translates verse 16 as 'redeeming the time.' Paul's point is that we must discipline ourselves to buy back our time from wastage. If we do not take definite steps, particularly

Making the most of every opportunity, because the days are evil.

because these are 'evil days' in which we are living, our time will be wasted. That was the case in Paul's day and surely, if anything, it must be more the case today?

There are so many distractions, things to watch, to read, to listen to . . . Many of these things are perfectly legitimate, but if we do not take special care, they will cause us to waste our lives. Two years ago we bought the Freeview television package. This means that the number of channels we can watch is considerably increased.

Up until then we could only get four channels and very often it was perfectly clear there was nothing worth watching and the television was switched off. But now we can flick through the channels and on most occasions there is something really worth watching. It is so possible for the hours just to drift away, as we watch material that is not harmful. It may often be helpful – but it has not been disciplined use of our time.

Time is the truly precious gift, and yet many of us seem to take it for granted. Seneca wrote; 'We are always complaining that our days are few and at the same time acting as if they would never end.'

The apostle James makes a similar point:

> Now listen, you who say, 'Today or tomorrow we will go to this or that city, spend a year there, carry on business and make money.' Why you do not even know what will happen tomorrow. What is your life? You are a mist that appears for a little while and then vanishes. Instead you ought to say, 'If it is the Lord's will, we will live and do this or that.' As it is, you boast and brag. All such boasting is evil. Anyone, then, who knows the good he ought to do and doesn't do it, sins' (James 4:13–17).

The gift of time

How often do we hear people, as they get older, refer back to an incident earlier in their lives, commenting, 'It only seems like yesterday.' Time is a gift given to us by God and to waste it is to squander one of his most precious gifts. In our earlier years, the thought of 'three score

Time is a gift to us by God.

years and ten' seems like an eternity. Moses appreciated this; 'The length of our days is seventy years – or eighty, if we have the strength; yet their span is but trouble and sorrow, for they quickly pass, and we fly away' (Ps. 90:10).

> Time is the deposit each one has in the bank of God and no one knows the balance.
> *Ralph Stockman*

The Puritan preacher Robert Wilkinson, however, puts this seventy-year time span into perspective; 'Take out the first ten years for infancy and childhood which Solomon calls the time of wantonness and vanity, then take a third part of your life for sleep, take away those days before you came to know Christ and any days when you have not walked closely with him and what remains is very little.'

No wonder Moses prays; 'Teach us to number our days aright that we may gain a heart of wisdom' (v12). He is asking God to teach him to live in the light of the shortness of life, to number or carefully calculate the time he has remaining. Of course none of us know that time, but we do know that there is an end to our lives on this earth and if we get to seventy or eighty, we will be doing well.

> Teach us to number our days aright.

What are our priorities?

If we are to calculate our days carefully, making the very most of our time, then clear priorities will be essential. One of the ways in which a true disciple of Jesus will be

> ❧❀❧
>
> **Tomorrow is a post dated cheque: today is cash.**
>
> *Anon*
>
> ❀

recognised is by the priorities of their life, which will be so different from those who are not seeking to follow Jesus. This difference in priorities can probably be summed up in the point made in chapter 4. The true disciple lives for two days, 'today and that day' while others live only for the day. The true disciple 'seeks first his kingdom and his righteousness,' in the confidence that, 'all these things' – food, drink and clothes will be given to him as well (Mt. 6:33).

Here we need to appreciate a very real problem. We live busy lives and the pressures are on us to do the normal things that our friends and neighbours expect us to do. We are expected to look after the house and the car and generally look after ourselves, our clothes, our

> ❧❀❧
>
> **Clear priorities will be essential.**
>
> ❀

looks, our health. If we don't do these normal things, there will be surprise and even scorn. But who is going to notice and be concerned if we are inconsistent in our prayer lives or our Bible reading?

Who is going to know if we go through another week without witnessing to someone of our faith in Jesus? Many sins are secret – who will know if we are failing to struggle against them? The great danger we face is that we live by the expectations of others: the demands of our culture rather than the priorities that we should set for ourselves as we commune with God.

There is a time for everything,
and a season for every activity under heaven:

a time to be born and a time to die,
a time to plant and a time to uproot,
a time to kill and a time to heal,
a time to tear down and a time to build,
a time to weep and a time to laugh,
a time to mourn and a time to dance,
a time to scatter stones and a time to gather them,
a time to embrace and a time to refrain,
a time to search and a time to give up,
a time to keep and a time to throw away,
a time to tear and a time to mend,
a time to be silent and a time to speak,
a time to love and a time to hate,
a time for war and a time for peace.

Ecclesiastes 3:1–8

I was really helped by the distinction Gordon McDonald made in his book *Ordering your private world* between the called and the driven person. I was driven for many years by what I thought were the expectations and demands of others, and I found myself on a treadmill, which felt as though it had been set to the maximum pace. It was exhausting and ultimately extremely unsatisfying. I have explained earlier how important the statement Paul makes in Galatians 4:7 has been in my life; 'you are no longer a slave, but a son.' Paul was writing to those who had been freed from bondage to the law and were in danger of going again back into bondage. I saw myself as

> I found myself on a treadmill.

in bondage and I couldn't be myself. I did what I thought others expected me to do and what I thought would satisfy them. I certainly was not free to serve God, I was serving what I thought were the demands of others and ultimately I was serving myself.

It was a huge day in my life when I got before God and asked; 'Lord, what do you want?' I then wrote on a card and placed above my desk a list of the activities that I believed God wanted me to be involved in. From then on, every invitation I received, however supposedly important or prestigious, had to go through a test. If I accepted the invitation, would it help fulfil the specific things I believed God had called me to?

Living by the expectations of others caused me to abuse the gift of time in another way. I very rarely rested. It is important as I write of the challenge to use the gift of time well, and to ensure that we have the right priorities, to look at what Scripture says about rest and leisure. The ministry of Jesus certainly led to a hectic schedule; 'Then because so many people were coming and going that they did not even have a chance to eat, he said to them, "Come with me by yourselves to a quiet place and get some rest" (Mk. 6:31). It seems there were great opportunities for ministering to people at this time, but Jesus is ready to leave it all for a time, recognising the need for rest.

One biblical principle I have consistently failed to follow properly is the Sabbath principle. The word Sabbath is derived from the Hebrew root 'Sabat' meaning 'cease' or 'rest.' If you study the principle of Sabbath in Scripture, you will find that God intended that for our health (and

Therre should be regular times in our lives for rest.

that includes our spiritual, emotional and physical health) there should be regular times in our lives for rest, and joyful celebration with the people of God. God himself set the example for us; 'By the seventh day God had finished the work he had been doing; so on the seventh day he rested.' God intends that there should be a rhythm to our lives that we pause from our normal work on a regular basis. If you look at other Scriptures related to the Sabbath, you will see that those times when we pause are to be occasions for joyful celebration, when with the people of God we remember his everlasting covenant with us.

> Even such is Time, that takes in trust
> Our youth, our joys, our all we have,
> And pays us but with earth and dust;
> Who in the dark and silent grave,
> When we have wander'd all our ways,
> Shuts up the story of our days;
> But from this earth, this grave, this dust
> My God shall raise me up, I trust.
> *Sir Walter Raleigh, 1552–1618*

Questions

1. Paul writes that we are living in evil days and in such days the natural tendency is for our time to be wasted. Are there any new disciplines you need to introduce to deal with the wastage of time? As you do so, how can you also recognise and apply the teachings of Jesus on the essential of rest?

2. Take a concordance and study what the Bible teaches about the Sabbath. Do you need to change the rhythm of your life in any way as a result of your study?

Books

Brother Lawrence, *The Practice of the Presence of God* (Massachussetts: Hendrickson Christian Classics, 2005).

Neil Hood, *Whose Life is it Anyway?* (Milton Keynes: Authentic publishing, 2002).

Gordon McDonald, *Ordering Your Private World* (Highland books, 2003).

Ideas – Make a chart showing where the time goes in your life – divide a piece of paper up into seven columns, and record what you spend your time on for a whole week. Then try to look at the same issues on a monthly and yearly basis. Then ask yourself some questions: What per cent of my time is spent watching TV? Travelling? Relaxing? Working? In real interaction with those closest to me? Surfing the net or playing computer games?

Then come before God and pray about the results and ask him if there is anything he wants you to change.

Chapter Ten

The gifts of God

You are a gifted person! It is vital to our discipleship to believe that. If we do, we will then seek to discover the gifts we have been given, do everything we can to develop them to the full, and then put them to use. But these gifts, given by a generous God for the good of his people, can so easily become one of the greatest stumbling blocks to the disciple. Many wonderfully gifted Christians appear to have been destroyed by their gifts, which have become the basis for pride and self-service. A striking example of this is the life of Samson,

You are a gifted person.

a man given exceptional gifts who simply did not have the maturity of character to handle them. In that state, he was 'an accident waiting to happen.' And the accident happened over and over again until we have the sad picture of this highly gifted man, his eyes gouged out and bound in bronze shackles, being used as an object of entertainment by the Philistines and as a reason to praise their gods. We need to appreciate and constantly remind ourselves that the natural abilities and spiritual gifts that we possess and the ability to develop and use them come to us from the risen Christ, for the good of his church and for his glory, not ours.

What comes to your mind when you think of spiritual gifts? I think many would think of gifted preachers or singer/songwriters. One of the gifts I appreciate, however, is that of our church accountant. He handles all the financial matters with a minimum of fuss and a maximum of efficiency. I can only stand at a distance and admire, realising that this is something I just could not do even if I was paid all the money he handles! The sisters and brothers who spend hours in front of computer screens in my office, developing programmes that I am able to use in my work, leave me equally grateful that they are willing to use their abilities for the kingdom of God.

Read the following passages and you will discover something of the range of God-given gifts mentioned in the New Testament: Romans 12:6–8, 1 Corinthians 12:7–11 and 1 Peter 4:9–11. If you are still at the discovery stage, I suggest you go through those three passages and make a list of the gifts mentioned. You will not then have an exhaustive list, but you will have an understanding of the range. Then seek to get involved, if you are not already, in a local church, as widely as you are able. As you do so, you may find that some of the gifts on your list are being used and in some areas you may begin to get the sense; 'Yes: this is something I should pursue further' or 'No: I just don't feel this is where God wants me.'

What can I do?

As you begin to develop in the areas of your gifting, you will find that others may well recognise your gift. On

Sunday, a lady who was part of the band at our church said a few words, between songs, to the children in our congregation. I immediately realised that she seemed to have a real ability to communicate with children. I sought her out at the end of the service and mentioned this to her, asking whether she had ever considered this might be one of her spiritual gifts. On the previous day I had been a guest at a wedding where the best man gave a hugely entertaining speech. I looked him out to suggest that he might well have a public speaking gift that could be used for the glory of God as well as entertaining people at a wedding reception.

Recently we moved offices, a massive job. It was done in a morning with incredible efficiency, organised by one man who has a clear gift of administration. That gift has been developed through many years in the commercial world and I am grateful that a few years ago he felt he should use that now developed ability within Operation Mobilisation. I am grateful because I am sure that if I had been responsible for the office move we would still be moving!

God can take abilities and training that have been used in other contexts and, committed to him, they can really be a help to the body. There is an important principle underlying this suggestion. God's gifts will often be discovered as we make ourselves busy in his service. Some have the idea that we shouldn't do much until we know what our gifts are, but it is better to get busy and discover God's gifts to us as we go. And please don't imagine that you will be always and only working in your area of primary gifting. I often

> God's gifts will often be discovered as we make ourselves busy in his service.

have to do things which involve me in areas of work which I am certainly not greatly gifted for, because the work has to be done. Though I still haven't been asked to do the church accounts! Surely in the body of Christ, if we are not prepared to serve in all areas, however lacking in glamour some of the tasks might be, then we are not ready to serve at all. And if we are not ready to serve in any and all areas, the questions might be asked, are we really serving at all or are we just serving ourselves, stroking our own egos?

Once a God-given gift has been recognised it needs to be dedicated, developed and used. It must be dedicated to God, because we have seen already the danger of using a God-given gift for our own advantage, and pride being the result. Simon the sorcerer 'boasted that he was someone great, and all the people, both high and low, gave him their attention and exclaimed, "This man is the divine power known as the Great Power"' (Acts.8:9–10). Simon became a believer through the ministry of Philip. He followed him everywhere 'astonished by the great signs and miracles he saw' (v13). Soon he was offering the apostles money if they could give him the ability to enable people to receive the Holy Spirit through the laying on of his hands. Peter's answer pulls no punches: 'May your money perish with you, because you thought you could buy the gift of God with money!' (v20).

It has been said that spiritual gifts are 'tools to be used, not toys to be played with.' If you use a tool as a toy, it can be very dangerous. It is vital that the development of our Christian character, which we have been looking at in earlier chapters, goes hand in hand with

> ❧◦❧
>
> **Spiritual gifts are 'tools to be used, not toys to be played with'.**
>
> ❧

our discovery of spiritual gifts. If we use our gifts but don't develop a godly character, our enemy can use those same gifts to destroy, rather than for their true purpose of building up the body of Christ.

Once dedicated to God, the gift now needs to be developed. This may involve training, it may involve being mentored by someone else who has the same gift and has been using it well for sometime. It will certainly involve using that gift in the church and seeing its development through use. What a different place the church would be if every member was actively seeking to discover, dedicate, develop and use their gifts for the glory of God and the good of the church.

A generous Giver

These spiritual gifts are, of course, only a part of the many wonderful things God gives us. It would take many books to even attempt to cover everything that comes to us as a gift from his generous hands. But I want to briefly mention three more gifts that I believe are vital to whole life discipleship.

Family life

Family is surely one of God's most special gifts to us. It certainly has been in my life. However, I realise that in this area I have been very privileged. Brought up in a family where I always knew I was loved, I have enjoyed the gift of a beautiful and loving wife, children and now

> Family is surely one of God's most special gifts to us.

grandchildren so special that it brings tears to my eyes thinking about them. I realise that this has not been everyone's experience, and have spent many hours over the years talking with people for whom the experience of family has been a nightmare rather than one of the most special gifts of God. I feel sorrow and anger when I think about this; sorrow for those who have suffered in this way, and anger that Satan should spoil something that God intended should be so beautiful and encouraging.

Family, for me, has had such a vital place in my efforts to live the life of whole life discipleship. It has been a place of encouragement and help when I have failed and also of constant challenge. I know that it is in the home, primarily, where the reality or otherwise of my discipleship will be seen. It is comparatively easy to play the part of dedicated disciple for forty minutes or so in a pulpit and even in the interaction with people after, but day in and day out in the home, the reality of it will be seen. Surely this is why when Paul writes to Timothy regarding the qualifications for eldership in the church, he states; 'If anyone does not know how to manage his own family, how can he take care of God's church?' (1 Tim. 3:5).

I believe there have been some very extreme views drawn from that verse over the years. We have certainly had family struggles and I have not felt that that immediately disqualified me from ministry in the church, but I do believe we can see here how essential it is to see our discipleship primarily expressed in the context of our family. For me, in a loving caring family situation, that is very easy. I realise for others it is a huge struggle.

> **Every family will be different.**

Every family will be different. Some of the Christian books on family life these days can leave people feeling condemned. If we do not conform to a certain pattern of family life, we may feel we are total failures. Families are, of course, as different as the personalities that make up the family unit are different. As an itinerant Christian worker, it has been my privilege to live with scores of Christian families over the years. It is absolutely true that no two are the same. I do believe that families that truly glorify God have two simple things in common; they see how essential it is to live out their commitment to Christ in the family and they make time to do so. They make time for each other: time to grow together in Christ, time to talk about their lives, their joys and their struggles.

God intended the family to be a place of nurture. I trust you will do everything possible to make your family such a place, and where Satan has managed to make it the very opposite, I pray you will experience God's very special grace. Remember that if things are not going well for you and your family, don't give up hope. The wonderful thing about the Christian faith is that it is a redemptive faith. We believe God is in the business of changing people, changing us and changing those around us. As he changes people, entire situations can change. Over the years, I have watched the redemption of many families, as people have realised their family life is not as God intended it should be. They have become unwilling to settle for second best and have begun to make change in their families a priority in their prayers. Having sensitively shared their situation

> ❧✦❧
>
> **God is in the business of changing people.**
>
> ❧

❦❦

In an increasingly heartless and lonely world, the church should provide a contrast of limitless love and trust. We must learn to bear one another's burdens and weep with those who weep. As God enlarges churches to impact society, we must never lose the crucial place of the small group network. As John Stott says, 'I do not think it is an exaggeration to say that small groups, Christian family or fellowship groups, are indispensable for our growth into spiritual maturity' (John R.W. Stott, *One People*, Falcon Books, 1969)

Terry Virgo, No Well-worn Paths
(Eastbourne: Kingsway, 2001)

❦

with others, they have generated more prayer, and sought advice from families they admired. It is never too late to start to change your family.

The church

Is it possible that if, for you, the human family has been a nightmare, God might give you a loving caring Christian family? The church is another of the great gifts of God. Now I know it doesn't always seem that way! Tragically, the church also has been a place of abuse for some rather than a place of nurture. For many it has not been a place of abuse but certainly a place of frustration. Chapter 12, where I write about discipleship in community, will show how vital a role I believe the church should have in our discipleship growth. I know that if I sat down and wrote on a piece of paper the people whom I would choose to be with on my discipleship journey, not everyone in my local church would appear on the sheet. But if my fellow church members were to do the same exercise, I know I would not appear on all their sheets. It is, however, a deep conviction of my life that these are some of the most important people God has chosen for me to walk the road of discipleship with – all of them! Those who are very different from me and who in normal circumstances I might not choose as fellow travellers have made a huge contribution to my discipleship journey.

I am very concerned at the lack of commitment to a local church that I see everywhere I go. When you and I became Christians, we became part of the Body of Christ. We need to be part of an expression of that Body wherever we are. This may not mean being a member of a traditional style of church, though we need to be careful of the view that the church has learned nothing in the last two thousand years, but it will mean being part of a group of people who are worshipping, growing and serving together.

Planet Earth

Families and churches have to live on planet Earth and this wonderful creation is a further gift from our generous Father. God has delegated to us the responsibility to care for his creation. It is only in recent years that I have begun to see the important place this has in my discipleship. I have learned this within the family, as my children have been much more sensitive to the voice of God in this area than I have. The debate continues as to just how much the misuse of our environment is the cause of such things as global climate change, though to a non-scientist the evidence for

> God has delegated to us the responsibility to care for his creation.

the damage we are causing seems overwhelming. However, the main reasons why we must care for God's creation are that it is his and he tells us to do so and one day he will redeem the world he has made.

Travelling as much as I do, it is impossible to avoid witnessing the consequences in other parts of the world of the way that so many of us live in the west. If we are to be obedient to God and if we are to care for our neighbour, even if that neighbour is on the other side of the world, we must take seriously the stewardship of our environment. So I have been learning in recent years a whole new way of living and I have still much to learn. The issues of waste, how and how much I travel, where

I buy my food, how I invest my money and so much more have become issues of discipleship for me. I often feel bad that for many years I had no understanding of the importance of these issues.

We are disciples of a generous God and we must recognise his many gifts: preserving, developing, enjoying and using them for his glory.

Questions

1. Study the list of gifts in the three passages mentioned in this chapter, and begin the process of discovering the particular gifts the Lord may have entrusted you with.
2. Consider your life in the family, church family and as a resident on planet Earth. Are there areas in where until now there has been a blind spot in your discipleship?

Find out more about the following as part of your attempt to care for God's Earth:

- Fair trade food, clothes, etc
- Farmers' markets
- Low-energy light bulbs
- Organic food, clothes, fabric
- Recycling initiatives

www.ethicalconsumer.org
www.arocha.org
www.traidcraft.co.uk
www.jri.org.uk

Books

Tony Campolo, *How to Rescue the Earth without Worshipping Nature* (Thomas Nelson, 1992).

James Jones, *Jesus and the Earth* (London: SPCK, 2003).

Rob Parsons, *The Sixty Minute Father* (London: Hodder & Stoughton, 1997).

Rob Parsons, *The Sixty Minute Mother* (London: Hodder & Stoughton, 2000).

John Stott and John Wyatt, *Issues Facing Christians Today* (Grand Rapids: Zondervan, 2006).

Chapter Eleven

Work

If there is one day for rest, then there are six days for labour! If we are to be true disciples, we need to have a biblical understanding of the place of work in our lives. There are some excellent books now available on this matter, and it is not before time. For years I had a totally wrong view of work. I saw it as a necessary evil, or at least a distraction from the true calling of a Christian. I went to work to put bread

For years I had a totally wrong view of work.

on the table, but if I could somehow avoid work and still put bread on the table, especially if I could do 'Christian work' instead, then that was the ideal.

I am often referred to as a 'full-time Christian worker' and I have to say often put on some kind of pedestal because I am perceived in this way. I intensely dislike this title. Clearly the implication is I am serving the Lord Jesus with all of my life as I go into the offices of Operation Mobilisation, or travel to some conference to preach, but my Christian brother or sister, as they make their way to their office, school or factory floor, are doing something different. Their work is not 'Christian', otherwise they also would be called 'full-time Christian workers.' They must do any 'Christian' work in the evenings or at weekends!

Who is the full-time Christian worker?

I used to work in the offices of a quite sizeable company. The chairman of the board of that company got to know that I was, as he would put it, 'a born again Christian.' He was fascinated and used to ask me from time to time to take the morning coffee break with him so we could talk. As far as I know he never became a believer, but since I left those offices and moved into so-called 'full-time Christian work,' I have rarely had opportunities to speak about my faith to those who are so prominent in the world of business.

Every day I walked into those offices I was surrounded by people who did not have faith in Jesus. Today I also walk into an office most days, and again people surround me, but now all of them have faith in Jesus. It makes me ask; who are the full-time Christian workers? Who is surrounded full-time by those who are not yet Christians?

The problem is the fatal divide we tend to make between the spiritual and the secular. A schoolteacher who taught in a large school in a fairly rough area of her city also taught Sunday school in her local church. She would, from time to time, get up in front

> ❦❦❦
>
> **Who is surrounded full-time by those who are not yet Christians?**
>
> ❦

of the church and give a report on the Sunday school work and then she was prayed for. She was never asked to give a report on her work in the comprehensive school and never, at least in front of the church, prayed for. She spent an hour a week in front of the Sunday school children and they were mostly Christians, or at least children of believing parents, and at least forty hours a week with the children at the comprehensive school who were, in the vast majority, not Christians.

Whole life discipleship requires a good work ethic. We need a biblical understanding of work, and to get that we need to go back to God. We immediately find he is a worker. Five times in the opening chapter of the Bible, he is described as a doer or a maker. After six days he rested from the amazing work of creation. But creation needs sustaining, so God goes on working.

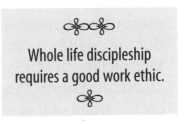

Whole life discipleship requires a good work ethic.

'He makes the grass grow and plants for man to cultivate – bringing forth food from the earth' (Ps. 104:14).

The Lord Jesus Christ, the second Person of the Trinity, is an important example for us. He was here for only thirty-three years to do the work his Father had given him to do, and yet spent some of those years in a carpenter's shop.

Without the work of the Holy Spirit who came to 'convict the world of guilt in regard to sin and righteousness and judgment' (Jn. 16:8), we would not be interested in being true disciples of Jesus today. When we follow God we follow a worker. If we are to be imitators of God, then we are imitating a worker.

We are made in his image, so Adam and Eve were immediately given physical work as their primary

If he (Jesus) were to come today as he did then, he could carry out his mission through almost any decent and useful occupation. He could be an accountant, a computer engineer, a bank clerk, an editor, doctor, waiter, teacher, farmworker, lab technician or construction worker. He could run a housecleaning service or repair cars … None of this would be the least hindrance to the eternal kind of life that was his by nature and becomes available to us through him. Our human life, it turns out, is not destroyed by God's life but fulfilled in it and in it alone.

Dallas Willard, The Divine Conspiracy
(London: HarperCollins, 1998)

occupation in the Garden of Eden. We were also given responsibility for the world that he had made. The responsibility to 'cultivate' and 'keep' applies not only to the land but also to everything that can

The arts, sciences, literature, everything is covered by this mandate God gave to us.

be cultivated or kept. The arts, sciences, literature, everything is covered by this mandate God gave to us. Some people dream of giving up work, moving to a beautiful part of the world and putting their feet up for the rest of their days. But inactivity satisfies no-one. A change of pace may be very refreshing and well deserved, but God made us like himself, to be workers and to take responsibility for his world.

Human work, along with everything else, however, was corrupted in the Fall. The curse meant that work was degraded and would now involve 'painful toil' and 'sweat.' After the Fall, human work had the potential to produce materials and instruments which could destroy rather than cultivate and keep. Soon a tower would be built as an expression of human pride and a community would be scattered and destroyed as a result.

Work-life balance

Today we know for many people work has become an idol. People overwork and often destroy their relationship with God, their social relationships (tragically so often including their family) and sometimes ultimately their health. I witnessed this when I worked for my former employer. I remember one of the directors whose commitment to the company was such that it destroyed

❧❀❧

In a recent paper from the Institute of Social and Economic Research, the suggestion was made that being busy is 'the new badge of honour'. Working long hours and staying late at the office is becoming a status symbol. This can be a subtle temptation to Christian workers too. Sometimes our drivenness and activism are the result not of the demands of our work, but of the expectation of others.

Jonathan Lamb, Integrity – Leading with God Watching *(IVP, 2006)*

❀

everything he had, apart from his bank balance. His family fell apart, as did his friendships, to a degree his health was affected, and then the day came when company practice meant

For many people work has become an idol.

he had to retire. He woke up the next morning without a life, because his work had become his life. Looking back, that man, who many would see as having lived a very successful life, lived one of the emptiest, most tragic lives I have ever witnessed.

In my present work, I have witnessed within OM and other Christian organisations those whose lives have been impoverished because their work commitment has been out of balance with the rest of their lives. I have, sadly, from time to time been one of those people. I have over-valued work and given it an unhealthy priority over other aspects of my life. I confused devotion to the organisation I was working for with devotion to God himself and I have often seen that confusion within Christian ministry. I will never forget the time when one of my sons shared with me that after he left home he had come round to see me in the evening on a number of occasions to discuss a very significant issue in his life. Each time he had come, however, he said he found me working or looking so weary, he just didn't want to add to my burden. I look upon this as one of the major failures in my life, up to this point, in my attempt to be a true disciple of Jesus. The failure was due to an imbalance in areas where the Lord Jesus had called me to follow him.

Rather than separating our work from our worship, our work should be an expression of our worship without it ever becoming the object of our worship. 'Whatever you do, work at it with all your heart as working for the

> Our work shold be an expression of our worship without it ever becoming the object of our worship.

Lord, not for men' (Col. 3:23). The particular context here is that Paul is writing to slaves. Even slaves, who would not necessarily be treated well by their masters, or receive any reasonable reward for their service, were to work well. I find the spiritual songs of American slaves so moving because they were composed not in a study, or a church building but in the cotton fields of hard labour.

What's my motivation?

What motivates people to work well? They like their boss, or their boss pays them well? Christian disciples must have a higher motive. If we work well it brings pleasure to God. We have probably all realised that our worship brings God pleasure, but we must see that our work, if we offer it as an act of worship to God, also brings him pleasure. That motive will carry you through even in a situation where you are not well treated and the pay may not be great. In fact, our light may shine most brightly in those circumstances . The way we work can quickly 'win the respect of others' (1 Thess. 4:12).

We do not leave 'normal work' to get involved in 'Christian work.' We do not leave 'secular' work to get involved in 'Christian work.' Those who come to me expressing interest in 'full-time Christian work,' because they want to do something 'really useful' with their lives surely have not begun to understand the biblical teaching on work. I have a colleague who, when people come to him with that kind of comment, responds, 'Too late: if you are a believer, you should already be involved in full-time service.'

Whole life discipleship demands that we see our place of work as a place of both worship and mission. This may involve a radical rethink of the place and purpose of church in your life. Many see the church as the place for evangelism. 'We need to get people to church or at least something like an Alpha course organised by the church if we are to be involved in effective evangelism.' There is no doubt that evangelism can be part of the work done in a church and thank God for the effective-ness of Alpha courses, but we need to see the primary place for our evangelism is with the people we spend the majority of our time with, and these days for many of us that is the people we work with. One of the primary purposes of the church is to help us

> Whole life discipleship demands that we see our place of work as a place of both worship and mission.

develop the character and the values that are going to shine out from us in the places where we work, live and take our leisure, and to teach us the skills of effectively sharing our faith with them.

Questions:

1. Do you see your work as something you have to do or something you want to do? Is God interested in what you do? Is he involved? Do you walk through the day with him?
2. 'Christians are not paid to witness but to do their jobs.' How do you react to this statement? Should Christians spend their working time explaining the gospel, or should they simply work in such a way that those around them notice the difference the gospel makes in their lives?

Books:

Darrell Cosden, *The Heavenly Good of Earthly Work* (Milton Keynes: Paternoster Press, 2006).

Mark Greene, *Thank God It's Monday* (Bletchley: Scripture Union, 2001).

Neil Hood, *God's Payroll: Whose Work Is It Anyway?* (Milton Keynes: Authentic Publishing, 2003).

David Oliver, *Work – Prison or Place of Destiny?* (Milton Keynes: Authentic Publishing, 2002).

Part Three

The tools of
the trade

Chapter Twelve

Discipleship in community

I was born and brought up in the western world, a culture where individualism reigns. I am not just western, but English, and worldwide it is known that 'the Englishman's home is his castle.' We are never more comfortable than when we enter our castles, pull up the drawbridge and continue with our private lives. As a Christian, I was brought up to believe that God was sufficient for all my needs, and I am certainly proving the truth of that teaching. But if God was sufficient for all my needs, then why

God might meet some of those needs *through* my brothers and sisters...

did I need to take those needs anywhere else? Why did I need to share them with my brothers and sisters? It never occurred to me that God might meet some of those needs *through* my brothers and sisters. . .

I grew up thinking that admitting needs and problems in my Christian life was a sign of severe spiritual weakness. For anyone to admit they were struggling with a period of depression seemed to be the very antithesis of being evangelical. After all, had we not been saved from a life of misery to experience the joy and peace of Christ? More than once I heard the whisper that such depression could only have a demonic cause! The popular testimony meetings I attended added to the delusion that the Christian life was plain sailing and if you were struggling, then there were serious things wrong with you. The words 'wonderful,' or 'marvellous' or 'blessings' constantly punctuated these reports. This all added to my problems because my Christian life as a teenager was far from wonderful and I was struggling with questions and issues, but felt I had better keep my mouth shut.

It is amazing how far we can stray from what the Christian life was intended to be. No-one reading the Bible for the first time would ever think that the Christian life was intended to be lived in a vacuum. Christianity is all about a relationship with God but it is also all about a relationship with the people of God. But the western culture in which so many of us live praises individualism and allows no time for vulnerable friendships.

> Christianity is all about a relationship with God but it is also all about a relationship with the people of God.

Such friendships can even be seen as a bit strange and questionable, especially if they are same gender friendships.

If, as is increasingly the trend, Christians attend church once a week, normally on Sunday morning, there is little opportunity for the cultivation of vulnerable friendships. We enter the church and receive a handshake; we join the congregation in song, are led in

❦❦

As in the time of the judges in Israel, so it is in the church today. Each person does what is good in his or her own eyes. If Christians today could recover even half of the profound New Testament understanding of the church as community, we would discover a powerful protection against the pervasive individualism that devastates the Western church … God's grand strategy of redemption does not focus on redeeming isolated individuals; it centers on the creation of a new people, a new community, a new social order that begins to live now the way the Creator intended.

Ronald Sider, The Scandal of the Evangelical Conscience
(Grand Rapids: Baker Books, 2005)

❦

prayer, listen to a sermon, join in one more song and are led in a final prayer. Some churches are changing this format but it is remarkable how many have not. Many churches offer a smaller group experience through the week but what percentage of the membership is taking up that opportunity?

When God created Adam he said; 'It is not good for man to be alone' (Gen. 2:18). The context is, of course, the creation of Eve, but there is a wider truth here. We are made by God to be relational beings. Jesus had friends while he lived among us and that was one of the names he gave to his disciples (Jn. 15:13–15). He developed a particularly close friendship with three from the wider group, and if Jesus chose to commit to such friendships, then surely I need to do so as well.

If Jesus chose to commit to such friendships, then surely I need to do so as well.

I suggest to you that if we are going to make real progress in whole life discipleship, vulnerable friendships are essential. Our growth will be stunted unless we develop in this area. I speak from personal experience, because here I have always struggled. And I am not alone. Various surveys have shown that, though this is by no means exclusively a male problem, women tend to be much better at sharing their lives than men. Men tend to have few, if any, real friendships, and

If you want to go fast, go alone. If you want to go far, go together.
African proverb

the friendships they do have tend to revolve around doing things together, preferably fast or all-consuming things, delivering us from truly sharing our lives.

The words 'one another' appear over and over again in the New Testament. Jesus did not intend us to follow him in isolation. The image of the body, which Paul uses extensively in his writing underlines this. Each part of the body needs the rest of the body for healthy development. We need the Body of believers if we are to grow; equally the Body needs us if it is to grow. Paul is clear in Ephesians 4:16 'From him the whole body, joined and held together by every supporting ligament, grows and builds itself up in love, as each part does its work.'

The goal of the church is the maturity of its members together: maturity in unity. This is Paul's point in Ephesians 4:7–13. Paul shows that God has given gifts and ministries to his people for the good of the whole, that together there might be growth to maturity. The goal is 'until we all reach unity in the faith and in the knowledge of the Son of God and become mature, attaining to the whole measure of the fullness of Christ' (Eph. 4:13). Paul is clearly presenting spiritual growth here as a corporate

The goal of the church is the maturity of its members together.

concept, though that corporate growth is dependent on growth in the individual members of the church. There is then a double consequence if we do not continue to develop in our walk with Christ; there is a consequence for us, but also for the Body of which we are a part.

This immaturity will be seen in a lack of spiritual stability. We will be 'tossed back and forth by the waves, and blown here and there by every wind of teaching,

We have a problem: it's called 'canteen Christianity'. People take a little of this, a little of that, they half belong to a church, they might try another next week, or they just go along to listen, not to be changed. Paul did not set out to make mere listeners, pew-fillers or spectators.

Nigel Lee, The Glory of the Gospel – the Keswick Year Book 2005
(Milton Keynes: Authentic, 2005)

and by the cunning and craftiness of men in their deceitful scheming' (Eph. 4:14). Every problem that comes across our path will cause us to question the faith that we have embraced. 'Can God really be good if he allows this to happen to me?' The latest popular preachers, best-selling book or the most recent conference we have visited will bring a fresh burst of enthusiasm, but not for very long.

What is the answer? How can we move on to greater maturity and stability? The question is urgent because it appears that so many Christians live at this level. They are vulnerable to the devil's schemes, and their rollercoaster lives do not attract others to the faith. Is it not also the case that caring for Christians who stay at this level takes a massive amount of time from other Christians, who could use their energies to reach out to many more that have no faith?

Paul writes that truth and love are essential if we are to encourage one another forward to greater maturity. 'Speaking the truth in love we will in all things grow up into him who is the head, that is Christ.' The Greek verb Paul uses refers to much more than speaking; we must 'live out the truth' before one another. Authentic relationships are crucial to our growth into maturity as Christ's disciples. Our growth will be stunted unless we develop in this area.

A few years ago, my family helped me to realise that my life was out of balance. I was extremely busy, so much so that some of the essential things of life were being missed or at least not getting the time they should get. Family, as is so often the case, was one of

> I needed to build into my life two things, solitude and friendship.

One of the characteristics of genuine Christian fellowship in our churches or organisations will be open hearts. We can usually tell that this is a feature of healthy community by such practical signs as open homes, not formal relationships; open fellowship, not special in-groups; open communication which confronts as well as encourages, not innuendo and gossip . . . Opening our hearts wide is an essential part of Christian integrity and represents an attractive feature of Christian community which commends the gospel in an age of fractured relationships.

Jonathan Lamb, Integrity – Leading with God Watching *(Leicester: IVP, 2006)* those things. As I reviewed my life I saw that I needed to make a number of changes. I saw that I needed to build into my life two things, solitude and friendships. I will mention the importance of solitude in chapter 13 but I also realised that though I had many acquaintances, I had very few what I now call fruitful friendships. We must have relationships where we really care for one another, care enough to encourage and, where necessary, to confront. Our churches should be places where such relationships develop.

In 1 Thessalonians 5:12–14, Paul is exhorting the believers to actions which would make for truly healthy church life. 'Now we ask you, brothers, to respect those who work hard among you, who are over you in the Lord and who admonish you. Hold them in the highest regard in love because of their work. Live in peace with each other. And we urge you, brothers, warn those who are idle, encourage the timid, help the weak, be patient with everyone.' Paul wants a church where there is respect for leadership, because the leadership works hard for the people, but not a church where the members leave everything to the leadership and then complain when everything is not done. He looks for a church where not only the leaders care for the people but there is mutual care, and real care: warning as well as encouraging.

It is encouraging to see a growth in what many call accountability groups in my own church and, I believe, in many churches. It is normally best if these are single sex groups; safe places where there is clear understanding of how information shared will be handled, places where we can open up with one another, encourage and hold each other accountable. Some men that I know resist such relationships, arguing that their wives fill this role and they are accountable to them. Certainly the relationship we have with our spouse should be the most intimate in our lives, but I believe men also need male relationships with those who, for example, understand their sexual drives and temptations and can hold them accountable. Women assure me that same sex relationships are equally important for them. I think if we could see even more growth in this practice it would be one of the most hopeful signs for the body of Christ around the world.

Questions

1. Do you have friendships which encourage you in your walk with Christ? How can you strengthen and develop those relationships? And do you encourage others?
2. If you don't have such relationships at the moment, what can you do to develop them?

Books

Simon Jones, *Building a Better Body* (Milton Keynes: Authentic, 2007).
John Stott, *The Living Church* (Leicester: IVP, 2007).

www.menofintegrity.org

Chapter Thirteen

Spiritual disciplines

While growth in community is vital, there is no real discipleship development without maintaining personal spiritual disciplines. The two most vital spiritual disciplines for me have been the practice of the presence of God and maintaining a daily time to be alone with God in the most undisturbed circumstances possible.

The practice of the presence of God for me means living in the understanding that my life is lived before him; he knows all my actions, words, thoughts and motives. I am by nature an activist; my natural tendency is to rush ahead with things, to fix things, to get things done. It takes discipline for me to stop and reflect before moving to action: to remind myself that I have been bought with a price, my life is his and must be  lived for him. The work that I am called to and involved in (and I believe this is true for every Christian) is not my business: it is his, and therefore I must get my instructions from him. Added to my activist nature is a desire to please other people. I like them to be happy,

My life is lived before him.

and I also like them to like me, so the danger is that I march to the drumbeat of my perception of what others expect of me.

Without a daily discipline which gets me to spend uncluttered, focussed time in the presence of God, there is no way that I can ever live for God, I would be trapped in a life of selfishness. I need constant reminders of these realities; regular moments of solitude are a definite help.

For years I thought those who used the steam room in my local gym could not possibly be using their time well. From arriving at the gym, I could get a great workout and a shower and be on my way in seventy minutes. Then I began to learn the importance of these moments of solitude. I extended my time to eighty minutes and spent the last ten in the steam room reflecting on the day so far, reminding myself who I am living for and who has called me to the work that I am doing. I have just changed gym and my new one has no steam room so I will have to think of something different! I have built these moments for reflection into my day. The hour reminder on my wristwatch, for example, can be used just to remind me to pause and reflect. The coffee break, the cycle home from the office, certainly the first and last moments of each day can all be used in this way.

The most important time each day for me, however, is the longer period that I commit to seeking to be alone and as undisturbed as possible in the presence of God. It is a discipline I have sought to maintain throughout my Christian life, with varying degrees of success but never without a struggle. These times vary. When the children were young and the mornings were hectic, they were often brief. At this stage in my life I have more time to myself in the morning, and yet some days they are still brief because of the pressures of the day ahead. This

The first thing you must learn about prayer is that God wants fellowship with you and that he is drawing you to himself. To change the metaphor: He is pursuing you. He is waiting to trap you into an encounter with himself. He does so not because he needs you but because you need him. His is the tenderness of a mother over a fretful infant. Prayer is to turn inwardly (or outwardly – it is all one), enter the tabernacle where he waits and let him speak with you. For he is there. And he is speaking. And you may sit in quietness to drink in his beauty, trembling with joy.

John White, The Fight *(Leicester: IVP, 1979)*

morning, for example, I got up at four thirty to get a taxi to the airport for an early morning flight; my quiet time today has been very different from those earlier in the week when I didn't need to be in my office until nine o'clock.

I mention this because there was a time in my life when the quiet time was a burden rather than a blessing. I had a set view of what a true quiet time must be, and if I didn't achieve it every day, then a degree of guilt was the result. That hardly sounds like a love relationship. But there have been other times when the discipline has slipped, and without those regular times, I am soon living the selfish life once again.

> Without those regular times, I m soon living the selfish life once again.

Do you have a regular quiet time? If not, I want to challenge you to start immediately and persevere. It is a strange thing that we need to be challenged to do this. Surely this is the greatest privilege of our lives? We must never forget the cost that was paid in order that we might enjoy this privilege. I believe a great deal of what we have been looking at in this book so far will be impacted by this regular appointment with God. So often in my time with God I have realised that I have been planning to do something later in the day and my motives or attitudes have been wrong. I have also realised that, on another issue, my perspective has been a 'this world' perspective and I need to look again at the issue with eternity in view.

I do not always come away from such times feeling I have had a thrilling time hearing from God through his word, and having had a sense of intimate communion with him, but I have never regretted that this has become the regular discipline of my life.

You may think I have down played discipline a little so far. This is where I have needed discipline more than anywhere else in my discipleship development, the discipline to do those things that I know I must do if I am going to walk closely with God, things that often, at the time, I do not want to do. Sometimes my whole selfish nature seeks to convince me not to do them. . .

I have a chair in my study that has become a very important place for me. It is the place where, when I am home, I have my morning quiet time. The aids that I use in that quiet time are on the desk alongside. That place is no more sacred than the kitchen sink downstairs, but it has become a sacred place for me. Sometimes it is an enormous struggle just to get there. Life for most people reading this book is hectic, I imagine, and it very easily gets cluttered. It is much the same for me.

When I get to that chair, I then have to prepare myself for worship. I have very deliberately to try and deal with the clutter which can so often fill my life. This involves a notebook, because you can be sure that the moment I set my mind to worship, things that I have forgotten, things that I suddenly realise are urgent come flooding into my mind. I write them in the notebook to be dealt with later, the urgent not too much later! Sadly, sometimes other things come into my mind, such as those whom I may have offended, in the rush of life, without even realising it. Now, in the stillness, the truth begins to dawn. I write their names in the book, or sometimes I have to pick up the telephone and take immediate action. And then promises I have made but failed to fulfil sometimes come to mind, and I have to seek forgiveness and again take the notebook so that I won't forget again. I have to confess that sometimes I

come away with the notebook so full that there is a
day's work contained in it!

This chair I sit on is one that Win bought for me one
Christmas. It is a recliner. I like to recline that chair when
I am praying and meditate on the fact that I can rest in
the arms of Jesus, meditate on his love for me and his
care and protection over me. Then I like to get on my
knees and bow before my Lord and submit my life, my
future, my family and my work for the day ahead to his
Lordship. Then I stand and
walk around the room for
a time, reminding myself
that I am going from this
quiet place to the hustle
and bustle of life, to be his
disciple and ambassador. I
also remind myself that he
walks with me, and that discipleship is just to follow
him. Occasionally, and even as I write this I realise it is
far too occasional, I will take an extended time and walk
along the river which flows through Carlisle or go into
the Lake District and, in the beauty of his creation, worship the Creator. Discipleship is a love relationship.

**Discipleship is a love
relationship.**

My quiet times are usually in the morning. I am a
'morning person' and I find it very helpful to start the
day in this way. This was one of the things that previously made the quiet time a burden for me, I believed
the true quiet time needed to be in the morning. But
sometimes I missed the morning and even though I
might have spent time with God later in the day, it
didn't seem quite right. Surely some time early in the
day in communion with God before the rush begins is
good? Over the years I have met many wonderful
Christians who just struggle to get out of the bed in the
morning, and aren't much use for anything before at

least their second cup of coffee, so if they are going to give the best time of their day to communion with God, it probably won't be the morning.

I have used a variety of aids in these quiet times over the years: the most helpful of which has been Robert Murray McCheyne's Bible reading plan.[16] If you use this regularly, it will take you through the whole Bible every year and the New Testament Psalms and Proverbs twice. I like to spend sometime reading

There are no rules.

through the Bible and some studying in detail a particular passage. But there are no rules. This is a relationship and anything that helps develop that relationship for you is what you are looking for.

Bible reading and study have always come more easily to me than prayer. I have had a lifelong battle to maintain a consistent prayer life. I have used all kinds of methods and plans over the years and some have been very helpful. Liturgy I have also found very useful in the last couple of years. It has given some structure and form to my prayer life. Prayer, like genius, has been described as ninety five percent perspiration and five percent inspiration and I would have to say that has often been my experience.

Some may not struggle as I do in this area. We need to recognise the place of personality and temperament in our devotional lives. The more introvert temperament may not find prayer as difficult as I do. Meditation and introspection may come more easily. But while we recognise the differences, our devotional lives must not be allowed to be at the mercy of our temperaments. It may well mean that we have to adopt a different approach, and the time will be spent differently.

My prayers of faith are not instructions to a well-trained God, sending him coded signals to dictate his behaviour. I am not insisting that God must, at my command, perform the miracles I need. He is not a circus tiger, listening for my whistle. I am, rather, coming to a good and loving parent, who always wants the best for me and has told me I must never be afraid, no matter how shamed, angry, confused or distressed I may be, to bring my needs to him.

Gerard Kelly, Stretch *(Milton Keynes: Spring Harvest Publishing Division/ Authentic Media, 2005)*

The quiet time – a regular appointment with God

- Find your best time and place.
- Develop a system to deal with distractions. Use a notebook to write things that come to your mind that might distract you.
- Reflect on whose Presence you are in and the immense privilege of that.
- Read a hymn; sing a song or listen to a CD. All these things can help us in worship.
- Remember this is relationship so there should be two-way conversation; listening to God, and speaking with him.
- For some, a structure for this time will help. The structure can be very simple: for example, adoration, confession, thanksgiving, supplication.

There are many other spiritual disciplines that will build on what, for me, are these two basic disciplines. I mention at the end of this chapter other books that will introduce you to some of these disciplines, but fasting has at particular times been very important for me.

When there have been really big issues in my life or problems that just do not seem to be getting resolved, I have found fasting to be a helpful discipline. My normal practice has been to miss breakfast so that I could give more time to pray through issues and to express to God through that act how important the problem was to me. Three extended periods of hungry mornings come to mind. On one occasion, one of my children seemed to be drifting away from his walk with the Lord. I resolved there would be no more breakfasts until there were signs of his return! Another occasion of considerable ill health for another of my children led to further hungry mornings, until I saw signs of improvement. The toughest time in my Christian ministry was a period in OM when, through one particular situation, the whole ministry seemed in danger of huge division. That was a deeply worrying time for me, and fasting was a great help and actually a great encouragement. I came away from that time with a renewed sense of utter dependence on God for the solution. I went to do what I could do to resolve the problem with the deep understanding that it was his work, not mine.

Questions

1. What steps can you take to build into your life regular, uncluttered time with God, if you are not already practising this?
2. What is normally called the Lord's prayer might be better called the pattern prayer. Spend sometime studying the pattern (Mt. 6:9–13) and see what you can learn for your own prayer life.

Books

Pablo Martinez, *Prayer Life – How Your Personality Affects the Way You Pray* (Milton Keynes: Authentic/Spring Harvest Publishing Division, 2001).

John Ortberg, *The Life You've Always Wanted* (Grand Rapids: Zondervan, 2004).

Colin Webster, *Time Well Spent* (Milton Keynes: Authentic).

Part Four

What is it all for?

Chapter Fourteen

Discipleship and mission

Imagine for a moment Jesus being your Bible teacher! How did he understand the Bible? What did he see as the core message? The disciples had this privilege. In Luke 24 the risen Jesus is meeting with his disciples. They are fearful and doubtful; 'Then he opened their minds so they could understand the Scriptures. He told them, "This is what is written: The Christ will suffer and rise from the dead on the third day, and repentance and forgiveness of sins will be preached in his name to all nations, beginning at Jerusalem"' (Lk. 24:45–47).

If we are to understand the Bible in the way Jesus explained it, we must see that the mission of God was that Jesus should come and, by his death and resurrection, obtain salvation for us, and then that the message of repentance and forgiveness resulting from his work should be proclaimed to the whole world. This is the mission of God, his eternal purpose: and it is the message of the Bible. The story of the Bible is the story of mission. If we are

The story of the Bible is the story of mission.

⚜

God was happy without man before man was made; He would have continued happy had He simply destroyed man after man had sinned; but as it is He has set His love upon particular sinners, and this means that, by His own free voluntary choice, He will not know perfect and unmixed happiness again until He has brought every one of them to heaven. He has in effect resolved that henceforth for all eternity His happiness shall be conditional upon ours. Thus God saves, not only for His glory, but also for His gladness.

Jim Packer, Knowing God *(London: Hodder & Stoughton, 1975)*

⚜

to be disciples of Jesus, we cannot ignore the priority that Jesus gives to this or the place it is given in Scripture. Jesus made it clear from the very beginning that one of the primary purposes of discipleship was the creation of missionaries. The call of Jesus to Simon Peter and his brother Andrew was. 'Come, follow me, and I will make you fishers of men' (Mt. 4:19).

And what a mission we have been given. The small bands of early disciples were given a colossal task by their risen Lord. They were still fearful and uncertain but their task was nothing less than global mission. They were to take the message of their Lord to the ends of the earth. But if they were now beginning to understand who the risen Jesus was, and the message he was proclaiming, they should not have been surprised by the extent of their mission: overwhelmed quite possibly, but not surprised. Jesus is the Saviour of the world, and his message had been that there was no other way to God (Jn. 14:6). If he were one of many religious leaders, then there would be no need for this global calling. Each culture could rest comfortably with their gods. But if he is the only Saviour, then everyone must hear. How could he ever commit such an essential task to such an unlikely group? What possibility was there of success? Surely the forces that would soon be arrayed against them would snuff them out in no time? How vital that, when Jesus gave them this global task, he preceded the command with a statement of his universal authority (Mt. 28:18,19). He has authority over all who would oppose them. It is still the case, in many parts of the world, that the church seems to be a beleaguered minority, but the Lord of the universe is the Lord of his church.

This is the reason why mission must be at the heart of our lives and our churches. We need to be involved in mission because people are lost and unless they hear of the salvation of Jesus and respond, they will spend eternity in hell. Any Christian whose heart has been renewed by the Holy Spirit cannot fail to respond in compassionate action. We must be involved in mission because it is sheer disobedience for a Christian not to be. God's command cannot be misunderstood or avoided. But the primary reason why we must be involved in mission is that God has made his risen Son universal Lord, and every knee must bow to him, and one day certainly will. We cannot sit content while billions fail to give glory to the one whom God has exalted 'far above all.'

> We cannot sit content while billions fail to give glory to the one whom God has exalted 'far above all'.

Mission then must not be reserved for a special interest group in the church. It must be the whole church taking the whole gospel to the whole world. Paul has wonderful news for the Christians in Rome. 'For there is no difference between Jew and Gentile – the same Lord is Lord of all and richly blesses all who call on him, for, "Everyone who calls on the name of the Lord will be saved"' (Rom. 10:12,13). Then he asks four questions which give us the logic of Christian mission. 'How, then, can they call on the one they have not believed in? And how can they believe in the one of whom they have not heard? And how can they hear without someone preaching to them? And how can they preach unless they are sent?' (Rom. 10:14,15). For Paul, it was essential that a person believed in Jesus and called out to him, if there was to be any hope of that person's salvation.

So much for the popular and pleasant fallacy that there are many ways to God and it doesn't much matter

Jesus is the light of the world. We cannot therefore keep him to ourselves. We dare not attempt to monopolize him. Christianity is inescapably and unashamedly a missionary faith.'

John Stott, Authentic Christianity
(Leicester: IVP, 1995)

which way you choose, as long as you follow it sincerely. But people are not going to believe or call out to Jesus unless they hear about him. Millions still in our world have not heard a clear presentation of who Jesus is and what he has done. Over two thousand years ago, Jesus said; 'Go and tell.' Over two thousand years later millions still wait to hear. And they are not all in Bangladesh; many of them are in Birmingham or Boston. Surrounded by churches, they still have not been told the message of Jesus in an understandable way. They are not going to hear 'without someone preaching to them.'

You might immediately think 'I am no preacher, so I am off the hook!' Paul is referring here to the main means of communication in his day. There was no other way to get news around an area than for the herald to go to the city square or the market and 'herald' the news. The point is that the news about Jesus must be told, communication must take place. There are many more people hearing the good news today in small groups and one to one than from the pulpits of our churches. All of us are called to be witnesses, we are all to be involved in this mission. But some have a special call to front line communication. God may call them to make the communication of this message their paid occupation. But 'How can they preach unless they are sent?' Thank God for those he calls to be senders, to enable people to have this full-time calling, by their faithful commitment to make money and to use that money for the kingdom, rather than selfishly.

> **The news about Jesus must be told.**

When I was a child, I always looked forward to the missionary weekend in our church. To be honest, the services in the church that weekend were a bit more interesting than the services the other fifty-one weeks. Exciting stories from Africa, India, Latin America and elsewhere would sometimes keep my attention. But it is interesting as I look back on those weekends today. As I grew up, I had the feeling that mission must be something the church thinks about once a year. I believed it was an 'any other business item' on the church's agenda, not at the core of what the church was all about. I also began to understand that these missionaries, when they spoke about mission, so often seemed to turn to one of three or four passages. The end of Matthew 28 was often read, as was the end of Matthew 9 and sometimes this passage we have just considered in Romans 10. So my feeling grew. Not only is mission something the church thinks about once a year, it is something the Bible mentions only three or four times. No wonder the church only mentions it once a year!

The story of mission is one of the great and central themes of the Bible. It begins with creation. Creation tells us about the Creator. There is one God; he is Almighty, Sovereign over his creation. We can see in the creation story that he is not a God of wood or stone but a living communicating Being. But mission cannot be understood without the Fall. Evil was not part of God's creation. The Fall has spoiled the beauty and order of God's design. Not only has our relationship with God been spoiled but every other relationship has as well. So the way we relate to other human beings, our understanding of ourselves, even our relationship with the rest of creation; all have been spoiled.

The devastation of the Fall was followed by murder in the first family, the Flood and the tower of Babel. It would be no surprise to anyone if, after reading of this destruction in the first eleven chapters of Genesis, we then read of God washing his hands of humanity. The very opposite, however, is the case. The record of destruction is followed by the foundation promise of the Bible that will lead to blessing for 'all peoples on earth' (Gen.12:3). God explains exactly how he will bring blessing from this devastation. He has chosen a man, Abram, and from him will come a nation, and from that nation, every nation on earth will be blessed. Trace the theme now through the rest of the Bible. God uses Israel to be a light to the nations, then he introduces his perfect Servant, as Israel fails to fulfil their divine calling. Check it out in the opening verses of Isaiah 42. The risen Jesus then passes on the baton to the church – yes: that is you and me. And we even have the assurance about the end of the mission while we are still involved in it, as John in the revelation given to him sees people from every tribe, and language and people and nation (Rev. 5:9) worshipping the Lamb in heaven. John saw, by revelation, the fulfilment of the promise to Abram. This is the mission of God in which every one of Christ's disciples must play their part. I hope this helps you see that mission is not to be an added extra on the church's agenda but the first item, and every other agenda item must be considered with this first item in mind.

This mission is not just to bring a verbal message to people. We have no mission without a verbal message, but our mission is more. We are heralds of a kingdom, a kingdom we have already entered by the grace of God. We now, by the power of the Holy Spirit, live the life of that kingdom. It is a totally distinctive life, because everything has changed for us. Our motivations, ambitions

> ❧❧❧
>
> **This mission is not just to bring a verbal message to people.**
>
> ❧

and interests have been transformed. We used to live thinking everything was about today and this life. Now we know differently: we know that death will not be the end and that eternity with God awaits us. Everything is different and everything we do today, the decisions we make, are all in the light of the fact that eternity is before us. Our mission is to live that kingdom life wherever God places us. These kingdom principles we are learning will touch every area of our lives. They will certainly impact our lives in church, but also in the place of work, within the family, our leisure pursuits. They will impact how we spend our money, how we use the abilities God gives us, how we treat the environment in which we are living.

We will see that God is not only redeeming people but also the whole of creation (Rom. 8:19–22) and therefore every aspect of our lives will be impacted, and we will see that our mission goes beyond the saving of individuals. We long to see churches where this kingdom life is being lived in community, creating communities of grace and truth in the middle of society. These kingdom communities will not remain isolated, but be concerned to see the redeeming, reconciling, reforming message of Jesus impacting every aspect of the society of which they are a part.

> We long to see churches where this kingdom life is being lived in community.

This new kingdom life that can only be lived by the power of the Spirit of God will be a priestly life and will draw others to our God. The life of discipleship is a mission lifestyle.

There is a strange idea getting around the church that we no longer need cross-cultural missionaries. Some think the job of world mission is done, as they hear the great news of the growth of the church around the world. Others argue that the need today is for missionaries in the marketplace. Christians should stay exactly where they are in their place of work and that should be their place of mission. Thank God for the emphasis on this vital area of ministry in recent years: it is a high calling. Others argue missionaries may still be needed but not from the west. We need money from the west and missionaries from the growing churches of the Global South. It certainly is a privilege for those of us in the west, with the resources God has given us at this time, to help many into mission from other parts of the world. But let us deal with a number of the myths of missions.

Praise God for the growth of the church around the world: it has been unprecedented in recent decades. But with the population growth in our world, the number of people who need to hear about Jesus does not seem to decrease, even with all the growth in the church and the activity of the church. While there are areas of the world where the church is growing rapidly, this growth is not uniform. Large areas of our world remain largely unreached with the good news of Jesus. These areas of our world require cross-cultural missionaries who will give a considerable period of their lives to learn a language, gain understanding of a culture, in order to communicate the good news to a people who may never hear without such commitment.

> Praise God for the growth of the church around the world.

In some areas of the world, the church seems to be retreating, with the continent of Europe a prime and tragic example. What has changed is that these missionaries will no longer only come 'from the west to the rest'

Mission is our human response to the divine commission. It is a whole Christian lifestyle, including both evangelism and social responsibility, dominated by the conviction that Christ sends us out into the world, and that into the world we must therefore go to live and work for him.

John Stott, Authentic Christianity
(Leicester: IVP, 1995)

as used to be the case. Today it will be a global missions force, with, for example, South Koreans, Indians and Brazilians playing a leading role. However, we must resist the idea that all that is required from the west is money. If we in the west merely commit money to the task and not people, it will not be long before the money dries up. It must, as has been said before, be the whole church bringing the whole message to the whole world. Yes: the whole world; today when we talk about cross-cultural missionaries, it does not necessarily mean getting on an aeroplane. It may mean crossing the street. We live in a multi-cultural society where the nations of the world often seem to gather in one place, particularly in our big cities. Is it not also the case that in a nation such as my own, the UK, people have strayed so far from our Christian heritage and culture that to speak to them about Jesus also needs a cross-cultural approach?

So let's get started where we are. If we desire to be his disciples, then he desires that we should be 'fishers of men.' I know just how possible it is to be a leader in a missionary society and yet not really have the heart of a missionary. On the train or on the plane, for example, where I spend much of my life, I would much rather bury myself in my papers than seek to engage the person next to me in conversation. I have so few great stories of leading people to Jesus in aeroplanes or trains. Some people just seem to have a wonderful gift in this area: I don't! Some rarely make a journey without some great story to tell of a rewarding conversation. My conversations often never get past the

> ❧❦❧
>
> I would much rather bury myself in my papers than seek to engage the person next to me in conversation.
>
> ❦

person's occupation or family or the soccer team they support and this is clearly not my main gift. But I still pray for divine appointments and the skills required to engage with people in a way that commends Christ to them. And, from time to time, God gives me real encouragement.

Last week, for example, I flew back to the UK from Bangladesh. The first leg was Dhaka to Bahrain, and I was seated next to a major from the Sudanese army who had been in Bangladesh for a year. It wasn't long before we were speaking about being separated from family, because my work has involved a great deal of that. Then we spoke about the wars in Sudan and some of the terrible things he had witnessed and had to be involved in. We spoke about the folly of war. Then he was asking me why I had been to Bangladesh, and I explained my work with a Christian charity. He was a Moslem but now I was speaking quite openly and, it seemed, naturally about my faith. He did not appear to be offended but wanted to talk more and more.

From Bahrain to London I was seated beside a young lady who was taking a year out between school and university. She had been backpacking in Australia but was now on her way home for an interview to study medicine at Leeds University. She was very nervous about the interview. In my work I have conducted a number of work interviews, so I spent about half an hour giving her an imaginary interview. Then I said 'I know Leeds university: I have spoken there a number of times at the university Christian union.' At that point, she was polite but made it quite clear she did not want to go any further with that line of conversation. Sorry: no great success story!

We need to pray for a heart for people so that, wherever God places us, we will be concerned for those

⚜

Do you know when an individual Christian really begins the adventure of reaching out to other sheep not yet of this fold? It is when it dawns on the person that an evangelicalistic lifestyle is most certainly the will of Jesus and most certainly worth the risks involved. It is when a person does that cost-benefit analysis and asks, "What is the absolute worst thing that could happen if I start getting more intentional about my faith?" I'll tell you what the worst thing is, in this country anyway: someone might decline your effort. Someone may say, "I'm not ready to take that step," or even, "Thanks, but no thanks." ... I ask you, is that really so awful?

John Ortberg, Laurie Pederson and Judson Poling, Grace – An Invitation to a Way of Life *(Grand Rapids: Zondervan, 2000)*

⚜

whom we rub shoulders with, concerned to commend Christ to them: by our attitudes, our concern for their well being and, as God gives opportunity, by our words. The call to discipleship is the call to be 'fishers of men.'

Questions

1. Write down in one paragraph what you believe to be the mission of God in the world. What is your involvement in that mission?
2. The need to send missionaries to those who have not heard the gospel still exists – but do you know where it is greatest? What countries have the fewest missionaries? Do some research – you could look at *http://www.gmi.org/ow/*

Books

Patrick Johnstone, Jason Mandryk and Robyn Johnstone, *Operation World* (Milton Keynes: Authentic, 2001, updated 2005).

Richard Tiplady, *A World of Difference* (Milton Keynes: Paternoster Press, 2003).

Christopher J.H. Wright, *The Mission of God* (Leicester: IVP, 2006).

Part Five

It's impossible!

Chapter Fifteen

Jesus: the reason for it all

I wonder if that is how you feel as you come to the end of this book. Living as a disciple of Jesus is impossible, and I am so weak it is not even worth the attempt? Well, I have to agree it's demanding. If anyone else but Jesus made such demands we would not give it a minute's consideration. Imagine anyone else demanding that we love him more than anyone else, that we must be prepared to lay down our lives for him and that we must give up everything we have for him! Who has the right to make such demands? It is interesting that when Jesus called his first disciples, other than

> ❧❧
>
> **Who has the right to make such demands?**
>
> ❧

promising to make them fishers of men, he gave them no reason why they should follow him. He simply said 'Follow me.' He doesn't explain himself at all; nor does he give a presentation of who he is and what is important to him. He doesn't explain what he is going to do. He doesn't perform a miracle to win their allegiance. He just says 'Follow me,' and they follow!

He just says 'Follow me,' and they follow!

Jesus doesn't need to give us any explanation either, and he is not bound to give us any promises as we follow. He is the Lord of heaven and earth and he has every right to make these demands of us. He has a double right, not only because of who he is but also because of what he has done. Paul writes; 'You are not your own; you were bought at a price' (1 Cor. 6:19–20). We are debtors. We owe him our lives, and he demands our lives and has a double right to do so.

And yet though the call to follow demands everything, it is the call to life. The call to come and die is the call to life. The call that demands everything is a call to deep rest. Jesus said 'Come to me, all you who are weary and burdened, and I will give you rest. Take my yoke upon you and learn from me, for I am gentle and humble in heart, and you will find rest for your souls. For my yoke is easy and my burden is light' (Mt. 11:28–30). Jesus is speaking to people who had been weighed down under their often desperate but always failing attempts to keep the law. They would often have spoken of ' the yoke of the law.' It was no easy yoke; it squeezed out of their lives any sense of freedom or joy, and any hope of peace.

Now Jesus offers an entirely different yoke. He calls it an easy yoke. The purpose of a yoke is to help carry a burden, but this burden is easy. The word translated 'easy' means the yoke will fit well. Yokes at this time were made of wood, so the ox would be brought to the carpenter and measurements taken. These yokes were tailor made! The yoke of Jesus is tailor made for us. It is an entirely different yoke because, as we have seen, it is not slavish obedience to external laws but it is loyalty to a Person – following Jesus. In John 14.15, Jesus says; 'If you love me, you will obey what I command.' The apostle John writes; 'his commands are not burdensome' (1 Jn. 5:3). They are not the multitude of regulations of the scribes and Pharisees. God's will for us is 'good, pleasing and perfect' (Rom. 12:2). His will fits us perfectly.

Jesus places before us a choice and it sounds very strange. Imagine you were asked: 'Do you want to save or lose your life?' I don't think it would take us long to come up with the answer. Jesus said 'Whoever finds his life will lose it, and whoever loses his life for my sake will find it' (Mt. 10:39).

Jack Higgins, the author of such popular novels as *The Eagle Has Landed*, was asked what he wished he had been told when he was a child that he had not been told. He replied; 'I wish that someone had told me that when you finally get to the top, there is nothing there.'

When you finally get to the top, there is nothing there.

The apostle Paul, from his Roman prison cell, with a martyr's death only a short time away, writes to his friend Timothy: 'I have fought the good fight, I have finished the race, I have kept the faith. Now there is in store for me the crown of righteousness' (2 Tim. 4:7,8). Many would say that Jack Higgins saved his life and the apostle Paul lost his, but the evidence does not back that up. Someone else who said the same thing was missionary Jim Elliot, who died taking the gospel to the Auca Indians of Ecuador. He wrote: 'He is no fool who gives what he cannot keep to gain what he cannot lose.'[17]

To follow Jesus as his disciple is the only sensible response when we see the majesty of the One who is calling us. It is not a 'special' Christian life, reserved for the spiritually elite. It is not heroic; it is the normal Christian life. There is, as we have seen, a price to pay, but there is a greater price to pay for those who fail to follow. The price we have to pay is soon forgotten as we enjoy life as God always intended it to be, a life lived in close relationship with him, fulfilling the purpose for which we were created.

And we must never forget we do not walk this road alone. We have seen that we walk it in community with others, but the call of Jesus was to come to him, to be with him, and by his Spirit he remains with us sharing every step of the road.

He is with us to encourage us but also to empower us. I work for the missions movement Operation Mobilisation, which some would refer to as a para-church movement. This means that we seek to come alongside the church, helping it to fulfil its mandate to take the good news of Jesus to the ends of the earth.

> ⊰❈⊱
>
> **The Holy Spirit comes alongside us to encourage, convict, guide and empower.**
>
> ❈

Jesus referred to the Holy Spirit as the Paraclete; a word that means 'called to the side of.' That is the thrilling ministry of the Holy Spirit and surely there is no greater encouragement for us as we seek to follow Jesus than to know that the Holy Spirit comes alongside us to encourage, convict, guide and empower us on the journey. It is interesting to notice that all the functions that the Lord Jesus assigns to the Holy Spirit are, in other parts of the gospels, assigned to the Lord Jesus himself. It is no wonder that Martin Luther referred to the Holy Spirit as 'another Christ.'

So does this mean I feel the presence of Christ by his Spirit close to me every day? That is not my experience. I have days in my life when I know and experience the reality of Christ's presence and other days when I speak to him, cry out to him, and there seems no response, no sensing of his presence. I believe this is something that all Christians go through from time to time in their lives. If you have never known this, then you are unique in my experience. This is a day when we like to experience things before we believe them to be true, so when we go through times not sensing his presence, we begin to believe 'There must be something wrong with me.'

These difficult times can be made worse by dishonesty among Christians. We can give the impression to the struggling Christian that they are unique and that the normal Christian has a consistent experience of Christ's presence. The Bible gives a very different understanding. If you are struggling with this right now, it would be helpful to read through some of the Psalms. These are very real records of the experiences of some of God's servants in their walk with God – 'warts and all.' 'Why, O LORD, do you stand far off? Why do you hide yourself in times of trouble?' (Ps. 10:1). 'My God, my God, why have you forsaken me? Why are you so far from saving me, so far from the words of my groaning? O my God, I cry out by day, but you do not answer, by night, and am not silent' (Ps. 22:1,2). Read on and you will find the honesty of servants of God who often felt he was absent.

I've been walking with God for many years now with many days and longer periods of time when I have struggled to recognise the reality of God's presence, but as time has passed, I understand more and more that the

> **The lack of the feeling of his presence does not in any way mean his absence.**

lack of the feeling of his presence does not in any way mean his absence. Someone has written; 'Never doubt in the dark what God has shown you in the light.' It's a great principle. I know the reality of his presence, I know the trustworthiness of his promises, and the dark days are not going to shipwreck my faith. I am sure many of you have experienced that those dark days, though unpleasant, are so often times of intense learning, and looking back I see how essential they have been for my life and faith.

The promise of Christ is 'And I will ask the Father, and he will give you another Counsellor to be with you forever' (Jn. 14:16). He will be with you in the ups and downs; the dark days and the days you wish would last forever and he is totally committed to come alongside and help you walk the road of whole life discipleship.

It was the last day of the feast of tabernacles. For seven days, libations were made in the Temple with water brought from the pool of Siloam, but on the eighth day no water was poured. We are told 'On the last and greatest day of the Feast, Jesus stood and said in a loud voice, "If anyone is thirsty, let him come to me and drink"' (Jn. 7:37). It was normal for the teacher to sit, so his standing and speaking in a loud voice indicates the importance of his announcement and his desire that the maximum number of people should hear. And what an announcement it is. He makes the claim to the thirsty crowd to be the One who can meet their needs by the gift of his Spirit.

It is Campbell Morgan who points out that there are only two people mentioned in this statement – Jesus and me or you. The invitation is to come to him and, if we come, he will satisfy us with the gift of the Spirit. He will actually do more than satisfy us; 'Whoever believes in me, as the Scripture has said, streams of living water will flow from within him.'

Campbell Morgan also points out that none of us can ever know how many people are involved in that statement. As we come to him and believe in him, receiving the gift of his Spirit, not only will our thirst be satisfied but a stream will flow from within us that will touch the lives of many others. This is the call to discipleship, the call to come to Jesus; to be with him and to follow him, but it is also the call to receive all that we need to be satisfied and to be the channel through which others can be satisfied. Is it possible to be a disciple? Yes, by the power of the Holy Spirit – yes: and when God opens your eyes to see the majesty of Jesus, he is irresistible, so come, receive and join his community of followers.

Questions

1. We face opposition as we seek to follow Christ. That opposition has been defined as 'the world, the flesh and the devil.' What is your understanding of these three enemies?
2. Thinking back over this book, what three things are you going to do to walk more closely with Christ? Write them down and place them somewhere you will see them regularly.

Books

Alister McGrath, *Knowing Christ* (London: Hodder & Stoughton, 2001).

And finally, the story of a man who has lived a life of whole-life discipleship:

Timothy Dudley-Smith, *John Stott: The Making of a Leader* (Leicester: IVP, 1999).

Timothy Dudley-Smith, *John Stott: A Global Ministry* (Leicester: IVP, 2001).

Endnotes

1. Ronald J. Sider, *The Scandal of the Evangelical Conscience* (Grand Rapids: Baker Books, 2005), quoting from www.barna.org/FlexPage.aspx?Page=BarnaUpdate& BarnaUpdateID=95 <http://www.barna.org/FlexPage. aspx?Page=BarnaUpdate&BarnaUpdateID=95>

2. Ronald J. Sider, *The Scandal of the Evangelical Conscience* (Grand Rapids: Baker Books, 2005), quoting from George Gallup Jr. and James Castelli, *The People's Religion* (New York: Macmillan, 1989).

3. A.W. Tozer, quoted in *Gathered Gold*, compiled by John Blanchard (Welwyn: Evangelical Press, 1984).

4. Scot McKnight, The NIV Application Commentary – Galatians (Grand Rapids: Zondervan, 1995).

5. Scot McKnight, *The NIV Application Commentary – Galatians* (Grand Rapids: Zondervan, 1995).

6. Rodney Combs, Bonhoeffer's the *Cost of Discipleship* (Shepherd's Notes Christian Classics, B&H Publishing Group, 1999).

7. John Stott, *Evangelical Truth* (Downers Grove: IVP, 1999).

8. Josh McDowell, *Beyond Belief to Conviction* (Milton Keynes: Authentic, 2006).

9. *Esrcsocietytoday* – changing sexual behaviour in the UK.

[10] John Stott, *The Message of Thessalonians – the Bible Speaks Today Series* (Leicester: IVP, 1994), p.81.

[11] John Stott, *The Message of Thessalonians – the Bible Speaks Today Series* (Leicester: IVP, 1994), p.81.

[12] *Leadership* magazine Winter 1988, p.12.

[13] Quoted in Kent Hughes, *Discipleship of a Godly Man* (Wheaton: Crossway Books, 2006), p.22.

[14] J.A. Walter, *Need: The New Religion* (Leicester: IVP, 1986).

[15] Michael Duduit, *Joy in Ministry – Messages from 2 Corinthians* (Grand Rapids: Baker Group, 1989).

[16] To download a copy of McCheyne's Bible study plan, go to http://web.ukonline.co.uk/d.haslam/m-cheyne.htm.

[17] Elisabeth Elliot, *Shadow of the Almighty* (Milton Keynes: Authentic Classics, 2005).